lonely planet

PO

PORTLAND & THE WILLAMETTE VALLEY

TOP SIGHTS · LOCAL EXPERIENCES

CELESTE BRASH, MASOVAIDA MORGAN

Contents

Plan Your Trip   4

Skidmore Fountain (p60)
BENEDEK/GETTY IMAGES ©

Welcome to Portland & the Willamette Valley

Best coffee. Most food carts. Top craft breweries. Number-one hipster haven. In a city this open-minded, self-expression is met with a live-and-let-live attitude, and oddballs are free to take up space. From the hippie haunts of Southeast to the upmarket eateries and boutiques of Northwest, there's a 'hood for everyone here.

539 N W 13th

THE GADSBY BUIL
1906

Barista (p77)

Top Sights

IAN DAGNALL/ALAMY STOCK PHOTO ©

Pioneer Courthouse Square

Settle into Portland's living room. **p32**

IAN DAGNALL/ALAMY STOCK PHOTO ©

Tom McCall Waterfront Park

An emerald esplanade of activity. **p30**

Alberta Arts District

Portland's multi-cultural creative hub. **p84**

Powell's City of Books

A city block of books. **p68**

Craft Beer in Southeast Portland

Best for Beervana's unique brews. **p102**

MAXYM/SHUTTERSTOCK ©

LEFT: EQROY/SHUTTERSTOCK © RIGHT: JON BILOUS/SHUTTERSTOCK ©

Saturday Market

Portland's bizarre local bazaar.
p54

Lan Su Chinese Garden

An oasis of Chinese traditions.
p52

Forest Park

An enchanting urban wilderness. **p80**

Washington Park

An idyllic hillside retreat. **p48**

LEFT: DANITA DELIMONT/GETTY IMAGES ©; RIGHT: MARK TURNER/GETTY IMAGES ©

JEREMY JANUS PHOTOGRAPHY/SHUTTERSTOCK ©

Columbia River Gorge

Waterfalls, forests and a mighty big river. **p116**

Eating

Expect everything from food carts and fast casual joints to upmarket establishments and experimental, multicourse eateries. The city's chefs have an arsenal of fresh, seasonal ingredients – meaning even the most humble dishes are top quality.

Street Food

Some of Portland's most amazing food comes from humble little kitchens-on-wheels. Found all over town clumped together in parking lots or otherwise un-occupied spaces, food carts offer hungry wanderers a chance to try unusual dishes at low prices, and they often have covered seating areas if you don't like to walk while you eat. Many of Portland's beloved eateries got their start as food carts, with specialties that were such hits that brick-and-mortar locations were established to serve increasing demands.

Brunch

Portlanders love brunch and are willing to wait in long lines to get it. At the most popular places, it's not unheard of to arrive when the restaurant opens and learn that you face a two-hour wait. Weekend hours are usually from 9am to 2pm; some places are open only Satur-day and Sunday.

Fine Dining

Portland is nationally recognized for its food scene, with dozens of young, top-notch chefs pushing the boundaries of ethnic and regional cuisines and making the most of locally sourced, sustainably raised ingredients. Fairly casual clothes are acceptable even at higher-end places, where reservations are a good idea.

Best Brunch

Screen Door Withstand the infamous queue and then reward yourself with

STEVE TERRILL/JAYNES GALLERY/DANITADELIMONT.COM/AGEFOTOSTOCK ©

Southern-fried goodness like chicken and waffles. (p99)

Pine State Biscuits Mammoth Southern-style biscuit breakfast sandwiches with decadent adornments like fried chicken. (p91)

Tasty n Daughters Serves favorites like *shakshuka* and *patatas bravas*, and a *pide* breakfast pizza. (p110)

Best Upmarket

Le Pigeon Portland's favorite French restaurant offers a comprehensive experience with a seven-course tasting menu. (p111)

Imperial Renowned chef Vitaly Paley nails new American cuisine at this upscale hotel joint. (p44)

Ataula Upmarket eatery offering a modern take on traditional Spanish tapas. (p76)

Best International Fare

Akadi PDX Authentic West African dishes prepared by a chef from the Ivory Coast. (p91)

Kachka Traditional Russian dishes served with a side of Soviet kitsch in this homey space. (p110)

Pok Pok Chef Andy Ricker's famous Thai street-food restaurant serving favorites like Ike's chicken wings. (p110)

Best Pacific Northwest Cuisine

Higgins A Portland institution, this elegant downtown eatery has been serving PNW classics since 1994. (p44)

Beast Thoughtfully sourced ingredients enjoy adventurous execution across six courses on this prix-fixe menu. (p93)

Irving Street Kitchen Pacific Northwest shareables with a Southern touch, served in an urban-rustic space. (p76)

Drinking & Nightlife

Drinking, whether it's coffee or a craft brew, cider, cocktail or kombucha, is practically a sport in Portland. In winter it's a reason to hunker down and escape the rain; in summer, an excuse to sit on a patio or deck and soak up the long-awaited sunshine.

CAVAN/ALAMY STOCK PHOTO ©

Beervana

Portland was an early adopter of the craft-beer craze. Several of the industry's pioneers are still going strong, like the ubiquitous McMenamins, but new breweries crop up every year and most are well worth checking out. If you know what you like, you'll surely find it, as even dive-ish bars tend to have a pretty good tap list; if you're not sure what you want, head to any brewery and try a flight of different offerings.

Or just ask questions: most servers are well versed in what they're pouring and happy to offer tastes and make recommendations.

Coffee Paradise

Portland is full of excellent artisan coffee shops that take their roasting and brewing seriously. Even at average places, baristas know their stuff; your pour-over might take a while to get to you, but it'll be one of the best in your life. If you're a huge coffee buff or just eager to learn, try to attend a cupping session, or ask at a local shop about special tastings.

Cocktail Heaven

The 'bar' is as high for creative cocktails in Portland as it is for beer and coffee. Watering holes range from seedy dives to classy lounges.

Best Brews

Breakside Brewery
Experimental brews spiked with fruits, vegetables and spices, plus an award-winning IPA. (p77)

Hopworks Urban Brewery
All-organic beers made with local ingredients. (p112)

HEMIS/ALAMY STOCK PHOTO ©

Laurelwood Brewing Co
Kid-friendly brewpub with organic suds on tap. (p94)

Ecliptic Brewing Ambitious ales and IPAs named after the cosmos. (p94)

Cascade Brewing Barrel House Specializes in sour beers, many of which are fruit-based. (p112)

Best Coffee

Proud Mary Aussie-based roaster with stellar java and Insta-worthy brunch plates. (p93)

Barista This tiny sliver of a cafe was one of Portland's original third-wave coffee shops. (p77)

Push x Pull Bright, cheery shop with natural-process coffees and superfriendly staff. (p111)

Deadstock Coffee Sneaker-themed joint owned by a Nike janitor turned designer. (p63)

Stumptown Coffee Roasters This Portland roasting empire started with one roastery and cafe in 1999 and helped small-batch roasting go mainstream. (p63)

Best Cocktails

Abigail Hall Historic hotel bar with cozy, retro vibes and large-format libations. (p44)

Hey Love Hip hotel bar with tropical vibes, slinging tiki-themed cocktails and boozy slushies. (p113)

Scotch Lodge Cozy, subterranean lounge with some 300 whiskeys and Scotch-centric cocktails. (p111)

Departure Lounge Super swanky eatery and cocktail bar with stellar views from the rooftop of a downtown luxury hotel. (p45)

Shopping

KENNSTILGER47/SHUTTERSTOCK ©

Part of the excitement of shopping in Portland is that there's no sales tax. That combined with a number of indie shops around town that celebrate locally produced goods can make for a fun retail experience.

Books & Music

The largest independent bookstore in the country, Powell's City of Books spans an entire block and contains more than a million titles. But there are plenty of other indie bookstores around town as well as fun-to-browse record stores.

Wine & Weed

Portland has well over 300 pot dispensaries and more seem to be opening by the day since cannabis went legal in 2014. Not into weed? The local wines are world class. Of course everything in the city is sold with a creative twist.

Best Book & Music Shops

Powell's City of Books A whole city block of books – new, used, rare, small-press, special-edition, out-of-print and more. (p68)

Music Millennium This venerable record store with new and used selections is the oldest in the Pacific Northwest. (p115)

Floating World Comics Well-curated collection of comics and graphic novels, spanning multiple genres. (p65)

Tender Loving Empire Hip concept shop and music label with an in-store listening booth and records for sale. (p47)

Broadway Books Indie bookstore with solid nonfiction, biography and literary-fiction sections, plus regular author readings. (p97)

Best Wine & Weed Shops

Thelonius Wines Natural and organic wines are the focus at this shop that doubles as a tasting room. (p79)

Green Hop Hip-hop themed dispensary with strains named after artists who sing the praises of cannabis. (p87)

Pairings Select a bottle of organic wine based on your star sign or favorite rock song. (p115)

HEATH KORVOLA/GETTY IMAGES ©

Uplift Botanicals Friendly dispensary with knowledgeable budtenders and daily rotating specials. (p96)

Best Clothing & Accessories

Kiriko Made Atelier using vintage Japanese textiles to create clothes and accessories with ages-old techniques. (p64)

Frock Boutique Bright, cheery clothing and accessories by independent designers. (p97)

Next Adventure Score deals on sportswear and adventure gear in this outdoor store's 'bargain basement'. (p115)

Laundry Throwback streetwear from the '80s and '90s. (p64)

Orox Leather Goods Fine leather bags and accessories are handmade in this family-run workshop and showroom. (p64)

Ray's Ragtime High-quality vintage threads, mostly spanning the '40s through '70s. (p96)

Best Gifts

MadeHere PDX Goods of some 280 PNW-based vendors are showcased in this expansive Pearl District space. (p78)

Flutter Curio shop that reclaims and charmingly curates found objects, vintage wares and would-be clutter. (p97)

ZimZim Pop-culture novelties, T-shirts, birthday cards, tchotchkes and other quirky treasures. (p115)

Saturday Market

The largest and longest-running open-air craft market in the US, Portland's Saturday Market (p54) is home to hundreds of vendors, which are all chosen by a jury. Despite the name, it's open on Sundays, too.

Outdoors

TERENCELEEZY/GETTY IMAGES ©

Home to the nation's largest urban park, Portland's outdoor spaces range from vast and wild to manicured and contained. Wherever you find yourself, Portland's scenery stays green pretty much year-round. You can thank the rain later – and never let it deter you from getting outside.

Best Hiking

Forest Park The largest urban park in the US, with trails totaling 150 miles. (p80)

Hoyt Arboretum Twelve miles of trails span this garden in Washington Park. (p49)

Columbia River Gorge Less than an hour's drive from Portland, hikers are spoiled in the gorge. (p116)

Silver Falls State Park Loop through waterfall-filled forests in this huge state park near Salem. (pictured; p144)

Best Gardens

Japanese Garden A traditional teahouse, sand garden and koi ponds set a wonderfully zen scene. (p49)

Crystal Springs Rhododendron Garden Rhododendrons and azaleas reach peak bloom in May and stick around all summer. (p108)

Lan Su Chinese Garden Tranquil garden with a plant scavenger hunt guide. (p52)

Best Views

Pittock Mansion Unparalleled panoramas of downtown and Mt Hood from the backyard. (p81)

International Rose Test Garden See Rose City from the eastern edge of its namesake flower garden. (p49)

Best Parks

Tom McCall Waterfront Park A wonderful place to see springtime cherry blossoms. (p30)

Washington Park All-encompassing home to several gardens and cultural attractions. (p48)

Mill Ends Park At 24in in diameter, the world's tiniest park is reputedly home to leprechauns. (p41)

Best Wildlife Spotting

Oaks Bottom Wildlife Refuge Wetland refuge with birdlife such as hawks, coots, kestrels and widgeons. (p108)

Vaux's Swifts Each September, multitudes of Vaux's swifts spiral down a school's brick chimney to roost for the night. (p74)

Entertainment

Internationally renowned indie bands put Portland on the map as a musical hot spot, but a deeper look at the city's local entertainment scene reveals a coterie of diverse performers that excel in everything from opera to burlesque and heavy metal to jazz. And don't miss the ambient, independent cinemas that serve food and drink.

NICK GAMMON/ALAMY STOCK PHOTO ©

Best Live-Music Venues

Doug Fir Lounge Top indie acts perform in this subterranean, log-cabin-inspired venue and restaurant. (p114)

Mississippi Studios Intimate venue in a former church, with great acts and a fantastic, all-analog sound system. (p95)

Crystal Ballroom Historic venue with a 'floating', bouncy floor that feels like jumping on a trampoline when the house is packed. (pictured; p46)

Dante's Atmospheric venue hosting local and touring acts, with late-night pizza on deck. (p46)

Goodfoot Neighborhood joint with affordable basement shows and open-mike Mondays. (p114)

Revolution Hall There isn't a bad seat in the auditorium of this former high school. (p114)

Best Cinemas

Hollywood Theatre Art deco cinema with classic, foreign and indie screenings, plus 70mm capabilities. (p95)

Laurelhurst Theater Primarily first-run flicks that can be enjoyed with pizza, beer and wine. (p114)

Cinema 21 Single-screen '20s-era theater, showing foreign, art-house and classic films. (p71)

Best Performing Arts

Arlene Schnitzer Concert Hall Historic Italian rococo-style theater that's home to the Oregon Symphony and other cultural performances. (p47)

Keller Auditorium Home to the Portland Opera and the Oregon Ballet Theatre, plus occasional Broadway productions. (p46)

Portland Center Stage Portland's primary theater company, which performs in a state-of-the-art, two-stage landmark space known as the Armory. (p78)

Spectator Sports

Soccer and basketball rule in Portland but going to see a Timbers (MLS) or Thorns (NWSL) game at Providence Park is a wild and local experience not to be missed. Meanwhile, the Rose City Rollers roller derby league is one of the largest in the US. Hyperlocal to the extreme, the PDX Adult Soapbox Derby draws thousands of spectators to the slopes of Mt Tabor annually.

ETHAN MILLER/GETTY IMAGES ©

'Rip City'

Portland is a city of many monikers – some obvious, others obscure. Among the confounding is 'Rip City', typically used in context of the city's NBA team, the Trail Blazers. During a 1971 game against the Los Angeles Lakers, guard Jim Barnett attempted an ill-advised long distance shot that indeed swished, imbuing hope for a victory against the illustrious Lakers – and prompting the team's play-by-play radio announcer, Bill Schonely, to exclaim, 'Rip City! All right!'

Though the Blazers were ultimately defeated that night, and Schonely can't recall where the expression came from, he said 'Rip City!' each time the Blazers nailed a crucial basket or made an exciting play throughout the rest of his 28-year broadcasting tenure.

Best Major Leagues

Trail Blazers NBA team that set the record for most consecutive sellout home games, with 814 on Portland turf. (pictured; p95)

Portland Timbers MLS team with a cult-like band of devoted fans known as the Timbers Army. (www.timbers.com)

Portland Thorns Part of the NWSL, sister team to the Timbers. (www.timbers.com/thornsfc)

Best Homegrown Heroes

Rose City Rollers Beloved all-female, volunteer-run, flat-track roller derby league that's one of the country's largest. (p115)

Portland Winterhawks Junior-league ice hockey team, where some 100 NHL players got their start. (p95)

PDX Adult Soapbox Derby Costumed contestants in homemade, gravity-powered vehicles hurtle down Mt Tabor. (www.soapboxracer.com)

Art

ARTRAN/GETTY IMAGES ©

Portlandia-based cliche notions aside, this city possesses an earnest and unbridled creative spirit. It's evident in numerous art galleries and museums, plus a strong 'maker' scene where art goes beyond gallery spaces and museum walls. Take it in with festivals, 'art walks' or DIY endeavors that allow anybody with an itch to create to do so in an encouraging way.

Best Places to Admire Art

Portland Art Museum Portland's premier art museum including a wing solely dedicated to Native American art. (pictured; p41)

Center for Contemporary Art & Culture Pacific Northwest College of Art's space with revolving visual art and design collections. (p74)

Land Gift shop with an upstairs gallery showcasing original works by up-and-coming and established indie artists; the setting of *Portlandia*'s 'Put a Bird on It' sketch. (p96)

Compound Gallery Old Town Chinatown streetwear shop with a gallery dedicated to urban subculture and pop art. (p65)

Maryhill Museum of Art Remarkable museum, spectacularly located on a bluff above the Columbia Gorge, with a collection including sculpture and drawings by Auguste Rodin. (p119)

Hallie Ford Museum of Art Salem's top art museum boasts the state's best collection of Pacific Northwest art. (p144)

Best Art Events

Last Thursday on Alberta Art walk where indie artists and galleries put works on display for the masses. (p85)

First Thursday Art Walk Wander galleries and businesses downtown as they open their doors for new exhibitions. (p42)

Art in the Pearl Each Labor Day weekend, some 100 artists display and sell works at this juried fine arts-and-crafts festival in the Pearl District. (p75)

Best DIY

Pistils Nursery Hosts workshops on terrarium design, bonsai building and more, plus regular 'maker' trunk shows and gallery events. (p97)

Elements Glass Offers glass-blowing classes during the holiday season, when you can make your own Christmas ornaments. (p74)

For Kids

ALEXANDER OGANEZOV/SHUTTERSTOCK ©

Kids of all ages will have plenty of ways to stay busy in Portland. The city's wealth of parks, playgrounds and outdoor spaces are great for running around, and on rainy days, there are fantastic museums that are as educational as they are entertaining.

Best Museums

Portland Children's Museum Has a maze, theater, clay studio and plenty of outdoor play space. (p49)

Oregon Museum of Science & Industry Exhibitions, planetarium, movie theater and a submarine tour for all ages. (p108)

Oregon Historical Society Features a sprawling permanent historical exhibit with hands-on activities and games. (p40)

Best Attractions

Oregon Zoo Primates, penguins and African savanna animals in their own impressive semi-natural habitats. (p49)

Oaks Park Amusement park with go-karts, a roller rink and plenty of rides. (pictured; p115)

PlayDate PDX Castle-themed indoor playground with attractions for kids of all ages (and their parents!) (p74)

Best Rainy-Day Activities

Ground Kontrol Classic Arcade Bi-level arcade bar that welcomes all ages from noon to 5pm daily. (p63)

Powell's City of Books Massive independent bookstore with plenty of picks for kids. (p68)

Kennedy School Theater Second-run flicks in an old elementary school, with infant-friendly 'crybaby matinees'. (p87)

Best Outdoor Activities

Washington Park An expansive park with picnic tables and a playground and home to attractions like the children's museum and the zoo. (p48)

Lan Su Chinese Garden Traditional garden with koi ponds, a plant scavenger hunt and fortune-telling. (p52)

Salmon Street Springs Fountain Riverside fountain with computer-generated jets that are a blast on a sweltering day. (p40)

Japanese Garden Educational tea ceremonies, bonsai tree demos and koto harp performances. (p49)

LGBTQ+

With one of the highest populations of LGBTQ+ residents in the US – second only to San Francisco – queer culture is ingrained in Portland's social fabric. Most every place in the city is extremely welcoming and LGBTQ-friendly, and you'll see rainbow flags posted in the windows and yards of countless businesses and residences.

DIEGO G DIAZ/SHUTTERSTOCK ©

There Goes the Gayborhood

The Old Town Chinatown area has many gay-specific venues, but Portland is so LGBTQ-friendly that it lacks a definitive 'gayborhood' – so if you're here and you're queer, consider yourself at home. Venues that aren't LGBTQ-specific host queer-centric events like dance parties, bar nights, cinema series and film festivals. And if nothing directly catering to the community is on at any given place, you can count on the presence of at least a couple of other queer people.

Best LGBTQ+ Nightlife

Crush Lounge with an especially inclusive atmosphere and events like drag open mics and BPFQ (bi/pan/fluid/queer) nights. (p113)

CC Slaughters Nightclub with a bumping dance floor, complete with a disco ball. (p63)

Silverado In a city that loves its strip clubs, this is the only one exclusively featuring male dancers. (p63)

Hobo's Piano bar that's popular with gay men belting out show tunes all night long. (p64)

Best LGBTQ+ Entertainment

Hollywood Theatre Queer-centric documentary and horror film series, plus a monthly film festival. (p95)

Darcelle XV Vegas-style cabaret drag show, run by Portland's octogenarian drag queen icon. (p64)

Portland Pride One of the biggest pride celebrations on the West Coast, with marches, films, brunches and a big, gay boat ride. (pictured; p31)

Clinton Street Theater The world's longest-running screening of *The Rocky Horror Picture Show*, every Saturday night since 1978. (www.clintonsttheater.com)

Four Perfect Days

Day 1

Start on your adventure with a strong cup of coffee from **Barista** (p77). Once you're properly caffeinated, make a pilgrimage to the beloved **Powell's City of Books** (p68), then browse your way through the area on your way to lunch at **Tasty n Alder** (p43), downtown.

Indulge in some people-watching and take a mandatory selfie with the umbrella-holding statue in **Pioneer Courthouse Square** (p32) before wandering **Tom McCall Waterfront Park** (pictured above; p30).

After dinner at **Pine Street Market** (p62), check out the nightlife in Old Town Chinatown. Take in a drag cabaret show at **Darcelle XV** (p64) and then finish up with a nightcap and a round of pinball at **Ground Kontrol** (p63).

Day 2

On day two, lace up your hiking boots and take the woodsy trail through **Forest Park** (p80) up to **Pittock Mansion** (p81) to take in the epic view of the city. Have a well-earned lunch at **Olympia Provisions** (p76).

Make your way back up into the hills to **Washington Park** (p48) and its many gardens such as the Japanese Garden (pictured above) and International Rose Test Gardens, before winding your way to Southeast Portland for dinner at **Le Pigeon** (p111).

After dinner, catch a live band at the **Doug Fir Lounge** (p114). Finish the night with drinks under the vines at **Hey Love** (p113).

Day 3

JORDAN SIEMENS/GETTY IMAGES ©

Southeast adventures continue for day three. Rent a bicycle and grab a route map for a two-wheeled, self-guided tour of some of Portland's dozens of craft breweries in the area. Lunch at **Kachka** (p110).

Make your way further east to the Hawthorne District. Pick up a crystal or deck of tarot cards at a hippie shop, or try on some new threads at one of the vintage stores, then settle in for a movie at the **Bagdad Theater** (p114).

Stick around the neighborhood for an aperitif at one of the many restaurant bars, then chow amazing pizza at **Ken's Artisan Pizza** (p110) before dancing at **Goodfoot** (p114).

Day 4

BENEDEK/GETTY IMAGES ©

Begin your final day in Portland by taking in the exhibits at the **Portland Art Museum** (p41) then head to Northeast for lunch at **Akadi PDX** (p91).

Head over to **Alberta Street** (pictured above; p84) to check out the boutiques, galleries and coffee shops. Stick around for **Last Thursday on Alberta** (p85) if the timing is right, or head over to Mississippi Ave to browse more shops before dinner at **Ox** (p92).

When you finally roll yourself away from the dinner table, see if there's a live band on at **Mississippi Studios** (p95). After that, take your pick from loads of bars along Mississippi Ave, N Williams Ave or Alberta St for a nightcap celebrating your trip.

Need to Know

For detailed information, see Survival Guide p148

Currency
US dollar ($)

Language
English

Money
Portland is full of banks with exchange services and ATMs. Credit cards are accepted at most hotels, stores and restaurants. Farmers markets, food carts and some restaurants and bars are cash only.

Cell Phones
The US uses CDMA-800 and GSM-1900 bands. SIM cards are relatively easy to obtain.

Time
Pacific Standard Time (GMT minus eight hours)

Tipping
The standard in most circumstances is 15% to 20% of the pretax bill.

Daily Budget

Budget: Less than $150

Dorm bed: $40

Pizza or sandwich: $10

Happy-hour drink and snacks: $20

Light-rail day pass: $5

Midrange: $150–250

Hotel room with queen bed: $180

Nice dinner: $40

Craft cocktail: $13

Museum ticket: $15

Top End: More than $250

Top-end hotel with king bed: $250–350

Prix-fixe dinner: $100–150

Bottle of wine with dinner: $55

Massage at a spa: $95

Advance Planning

Three months before Make reservations at top restaurants; book hotel accommodations.

One month before Book food tours and classes. Purchase tickets for theater shows; concerts or Trail Blazers games at the Moda Center; or Timbers or Thorns games at Providence Park.

One week before Reserve places on walking tours and distillery or brewery tours.

Arriving in Portland

✈ **Portland International Airport**

The airport is around 20 to 40 minutes from downtown Portland.

Light Rail

The MAX runs from the airport to downtown (adult/child $2.50/1.25).

Taxi & Rideshare

Around $35 to $40 to downtown.

🚉 **Union Station**

Amtrak trains arrive in the city center.

🚌 **Greyhound Depot**

Coaches arrive here next to Union Station. Bus and light-rail stop outside.

Getting Around

🚲 **Bicycle**

Biketown (www.biketownpdx.com) is the city bike-share program; several shops rent bikes.

🚌 **Bus**

Trimet Bus has routes that connect downtown with outer neighborhoods (adult/child $2.50/1.25).

🚗 **Taxi & Rideshare**

Must be called in advance. Rideshare services are plentiful.

🚈 **Light Rail**

The MAX runs all over the city. Trains depart every 15 minutes (adult/child $2.50/1.25).

🚋 **Streetcar**

Lines connect downtown with the eastern and northwestern districts (adult/child $2/1).

Portland Neighborhoods

Northwest & the Pearl District (p67)
Hip high-rises of the Pearl District give way to fancy Victorian homes around Nob Hill, in this moneyed mélange of top-notch shopping, restaurants and parks.

Northeast (p83)
Ethnically diverse but gentrifying at light speed, Northeast brings together hippies, hipsters, innovative newcomers and long-time resident families in a wide variety of neighborhoods.

Downtown (p29)
Tall buildings, business suits, eclectic food-cart pods, people-filled Pioneer Courthouse Square and the best museums in town make this the bustling center of Portland.

Old Town Chinatown (p51)
Head through Chinese arches to this evolving, gritty part of town filled with urban street-inspired shops and restaurants, and hot nightlife.

Southeast (p101)
Thanks to its relative affordability, this creative-filled quadrant is a nucleus for everything Portland is famous for: food carts, beer, cocktails, coffee and freakiness.

Forest Park

Powell's City of Books

Lan Su Chinese Garden

Saturday Market

Tom McCall Waterfront Park

Washington Park

Pioneer Courthouse Square

Explore Portland

Scattered across five quadrants (with a sixth in the works) Portland's neighborhoods are unique microcosms of hyperlocal culture. It's almost as if the city is made up of tons of small towns that got stapled together – each has a distinct sense of community and special character.

Portland's Walking Tours 🥾

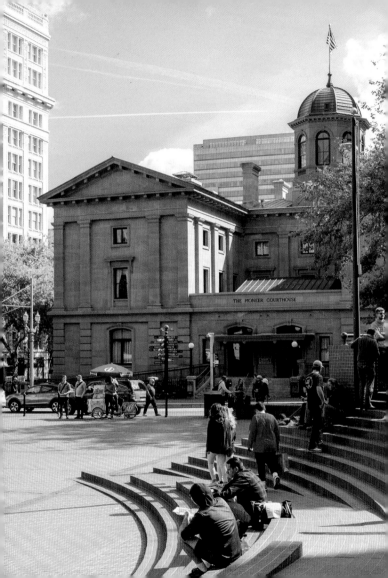

Explore ◉
Downtown

The workaday Southwest section of Portland is home to some top sights. It's also a transit hub and where you'll find the city's biggest food-cart pods. Several green parks, important performing-arts centers and plenty of top-end restaurants keep it even more lively.

The Short List

∘ **Pioneer Courthouse Square (p32)** People-watching, admiring sculptures and gathering for events in Portland's 'living room.'

∘ **Tom McCall Waterfront Park (p30)** Strolling an expanse of cherry-tree-lined paths, taking in monuments or checking out a festival along the Willamette River.

∘ **Cultural District institutions (p40)** Taking in art exhibitions, historic displays and performances at the city's top cultural institutions.

∘ **Restaurants and lounges (p42)** Enjoying creations made with local ingredients by some of Portland's award-winning chefs.

Getting There & Around

🚊 All MAX Light Rail lines (Blue, Green, Red, Yellow and Orange) run through downtown.

🚋 All streetcar lines (NS, A Loop, B Loop) run through downtown.

🚌 Most routes serve downtown; key routes include 4, 9, 14, 15, 19, 20 and 63.

Neighborhood Map on p38

Pioneer Courthouse Square (p32) ARTYOORAN/SHUTTERSTOCK ©

Top Sight

Tom McCall Waterfront Park

*This 1.5-mile-long park stretches along the banks
of the Willamette River and is home to many of
the city's events and festivals. Within the park
are several historical sights, and its expansive
paths – lined with cherry trees that explode with
blossoms in springtime – are popular for strolling
and cycling.*

◎ MAP P38, F5

Naito Pkwy

🚋 Red, Blue

🚌 12, 15, 35

This popular riverside park was finished in 1978 after four years of construction. It replaced an old freeway with paved sidewalks and grassy spaces, and now attracts joggers, in-line skaters, strollers and cyclists.

What's Happening on the Waterfront

The season kicks off with the **Rose Festival** (www.rosefestival.org; ⏱late May–mid-Jun), followed by Portland's **LGBTQ Pride Festival** (www.pridenw.org; ⏱mid-Jun), one of the largest in the Pacific Northwest.

Throughout July, beer and music festivals occupy the park, such as the **Oregon Brewers Festival** (www.oregonbrewfest.com; admission free, 10-token tasting package $20, additional tokens $1) and the **Waterfront Blues Festival** (www.waterfrontbluesfest.com; 4-day passes from $50).

Just north of the Bill Naito Legacy Fountain, an open-sided pavilion shelters the Saturday Market (p54) on weekends from March to December.

Cherry Trees

The Japanese American Historical Plaza (p60), just north of the Burnside Bridge, is linked by one hundred ornamental cherry trees northward to the **Friendship Circle**, a collaborative monument by sculptor Lee Kelly and composer Michael Stirling just west of the Steel Bridge.

Tom McCall

Named after former Oregon governor Tom McCall – a staunch advocate for environmental preservation and proponent for green urban planning – the land that currently forms the park was once the site of Portland's rollicking port. It was also home to the Portland Public Market from 1933 to 1942 and the Harbor Drive Freeway went through here from the 1940s to the 1970s. The park was completed in 1978 and named after McCall (who called for its development) in 1984.

★ Top Tips

o Get a great view of Portland's bridges from here, especially the Hawthorne, Morrison, Burnside and Steel Bridges.

o With its proximity to downtown office buildings, the park's peak hours are around lunchtime, between 11am and 1pm. The paths also see a lot of commuter bike traffic from 3pm to 5pm.

✕ Take a Break

The park's lawns were practically made for picnics – pack your own or pick up something to go from Pine Street Market (p62).

For a meaty meal with a waterfront view, check out LeChon (p62), located towards the northern end of the park.

Top Sight
Pioneer Courthouse Square

Affectionately referred to as Portland's 'living room,' Pioneer Courthouse Square is a nucleus of activity for the city. It is the most visited site in Portland and has hosted countless civic and community-driven events since its opening in April 1984. Home to everything from beer festivals to political protests, it draws some 26,000 people to its brick-laden steps each day.

◉ MAP P38, D4

www.thesquarepdx.org

🚆 Red, Blue, Green

The Weather Machine

One of Pioneer Courthouse Square's quirkiest sights is its 'Weather Machine', a 33ft-tall metal column crowned with a large silver orb that reveals the weather forecast for the following day.

The orb opens up to reveal one of three metal icons: a gold-leaf sun to represent a clear day; a silver great blue heron to indicate a drizzly or overcast day; and an open-mouthed copper dragon that forecasts stormy, windy days with heavy rainfall.

Finally, reminiscent of a mercury thermometer, a vertical display of light bulbs illuminate to show the temperature in 10-degree increments. An additional light system below the orb indicates air quality: green for good, amber for slight smog, and red for suboptimal conditions.

Events

Pioneer Courthouse Square hosts more than 300 functions each year. Its two brick amphitheaters provide seating for musical performances and events like Flicks on the Bricks (p46), a free summer outdoor movie series that takes place on Friday nights. Other recurring summer events include 'Meditation Mondays', a 30-minute guided group meditation; 'Noon Tunes' on Tuesdays, a series of weekly, hour-long free concerts; and 'Wellness Wednesdays', featuring an hour of free activities such as yoga, tai chi, Zumba and Pilates.

During the holiday season, a tall Christmas tree occupies the square's center, with its lighting ceremony taking place each year on the Friday after Thanksgiving. There's also a 'Tuba Christmas' event, which features 200 to 300 tuba and euphonium players performing holiday songs.The square is also home to the annual **Holiday Ale Festival** (www.holidayale.com; tickets $40; ⏲early Dec).

★ Top Tips

○ Check the live broadcast of the square (www.kgw.com/pioneer-square) to get a sense of the crowds during any major events.

○ During non-event times, the scene at the square may appear underwhelming – but it's a great place to take a break when downtown.

○ The Travel Portland (p152) visitor center at the square has a high-tech, all-gender, ADA-accessible restroom.

✗ Take a Break

If you need a quick pick-me-up, head one block northwest to Public Domain Coffee (p46).

For something stronger, the chic Departure Lounge (p45) is two blocks east and offers fantastic rooftop views.

Not all of the square's events are cheery in nature – it's also a key venue for many of the city's political demonstrations, rallies, vigils and speeches.

Visit the Pioneer Courthouse Square website for an events calendar.

History

Named after the adjacent Pioneer Courthouse, the Pacific Northwest's oldest federal building, the square got its beginnings in 1849 when shoemaker Elijah Hill acquired the land for $24 and a pair of boots. The local school board then purchased the block in 1858, opening Portland's first public school, the Central School. In 1890 the school was moved and the land became the site of the eight-story Portland Hotel – the archway and gate-work of which are still part of the square today.

The hotel was razed in 1951 to make way for a two-story parking garage, and in the late 1960s, developers proposed an even larger 12-story parking structure in its place. The city denied this plan, and between 1972 and 1974, they purchased the block, settled on its future as a public-use space, and instituted an international competition for its design.

In 1980 a Portland-based architect Willard Martin and his design team won the competition, beating 160 contestants with their plans for a multiuse urban plaza. But funding problems soon surfaced – construction of the square required over

The *Allow Me* sculpture

The Man with the Umbrella & More

Standing 6ft 10in and weighing 460lb, the **Allow Me** sculpture depicts a man in a business suit, holding an umbrella and hailing a cab. One of seven casts by artist John Seward Johnson II, the sculpture was donated for the square in 1984.

There are several other bronze sculptures throughout the square including five bronze masks designed by Willard Martin, the architect who designed the square (find them in the water trough next to Starbucks). And in tribute to Martin, there is a bronze replica of his top hat next to the top of the fountain, above the visitor center.

The northwestern corner of the square features an **Echo Chamber** – stand on the round marble stone in the center of the small amphitheater, face the steps, and speak out loud to hear a reverberating echo of your own voice for a startlingly fun auditory experience.

$7 million for land acquisition, structures and amenities.

City commissioners formed the 'Friends of Pioneer Square' citizens' group and raised over $1.5 million by selling bricks inscribed with donors' names (you can still buy one for $100), which would be supplemented by other donations and grant funding, plus a matching of dollars through federal funding. Four years later, on 6 April 1984, Pioneer Courthouse Square officially opened with a celebration that drew more than 10,000 attendees.

Designed for Living

At first glance, Pioneer Courthouse Square may appear merely as a plaza comprised of red bricks – but take a closer look and you'll notice architectural intricacies that reveal a rich artistic and historical significance for the city of Portland.

Framing the entrance of the visitor center is the **Waterfall fountain**, where water cascades down granite steps into twin pools. At the top of the fountain is a 'Keystone Lectern', which was designed to be a focal speaking platform and serves as a good vantage point for overlooking the activities of the square.

The square occupies a full, 40,000-sq-ft city block. Its center is laid out like an amphitheater, with two dozen steps arranged in a semicircle functioning as seats during performances or events. Surrounding the square is a set of towering classical pillars that progressively 'topple' in the style of ancient ruins. The tops of the pillars feature carvings of yellow roses with pink- and green-spotted insects, and some 'fallen' ones are topped with bronze chess boards.

Walking Tour 🥾

Downtown Stroll

Stroll the heart of Portland from Pioneer Courthouse Square, the city's 'living room,' to museums, Portland State University, open markets, fountains and of course the banks of the lovely Willamette River. Along the way pay homage to the Goddess of Commerce and the city's Japanese heritage.

Walk Facts

Start Pioneer Courthouse Square (🚃 Red, Blue, Green)

End Japanese American Historical Plaza (🚃 Red, Blue)

Length 2.2 miles; 1½ hours

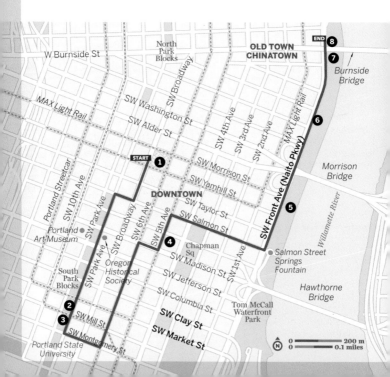

❶ Weather Machine

Begin your exploration at **Pioneer Courthouse Square** (p32), and get a forecast from the square's 33ft-tall 'Weather Machine' beacon at noon everyday.

❷ Trees, art & history

From there, head two blocks south along Broadway, then pop over a block on SW Salmon St to the **South Park Blocks** (p40), a 12-block-long greenway. Stroll along the leafy paths, with eyes out for the **Portland Art Museum** (p41) and the **Oregon Historical Society** (p40) on either side of the esplanade.

❸ Shop the University

If you catch yourself in the area on a Saturday, the farmers market at **Portland State University** (p40) is worth walking south to SW Montgomery St. Here, more than 100 vendors sell produce and freshly prepared goodies, and you'll also find a variety of food carts.

❹ Portlandia

From there, make your way northeast to the **Portland Building** (p40) on SW 5th Ave between SW Madison and SW Main Sts. It's worth passing for a glimpse of **Portlandia**, a 34ft bronze statute of Portland's supposed patroness, the Goddess of Commerce – it's the second-largest hammered-copper statue in the country after the Statue of Liberty.

❺ Waterfront parks

Head a block north to SW Salmon St and turn right to continue to **Tom McCall Waterfront Park** (p30). Stop at the interactive **Salmon Street Springs Fountain** (p40), which jets water to the beat of computer-generated patterns. A block north is **Mill Ends Park** (p41) – the smallest public park in the world, and the supposed home of leprechauns.

❻ Battleship Oregon

Cross back into Tom McCall park and continue north along the paved waterfront path. Pass the Morrison Bridge to reach the **Battleship Oregon Memorial** – the time capsule inscription at the base of the monument was sealed in 1976 and will be opened in 2076.

❼ To Market

If it's a weekend, you'll be lured near the Burnside Bridge to the **Saturday Market** (p54), where hundreds of local vendors sell everything from art and kitschy souvenirs to clothing and handmade accessories.

❽ Japanese American Art

North of the Burnside Bridge is the **Japanese American Historical Plaza** (p60), which features art dedicated to the Pacific Northwest's Japanese immigrants and native US citizens of Japanese descent who were sent to internment camps during WWII. Cherry trees lead you north to the **Friendship Circle**, an interactive monument playing Japanese music.

Downtown

OLD TOWN
CHINATOWN

North
Park
Blocks

NW 2nd Ave
NW 3rd Ave
NW 4th Ave
NW Couch St
NW Couch St
NW 6th Ave
NW Broadway
NW 8th Ave
NW Park Ave
NW 9th Ave
NW 10th Ave
NW 11th Ave
NW 12th Ave
NW 13th Ave
NW 14th Ave

W Burnside St

SW Ankeny St
SW Ash St
SW Pine St
SW Oak St
SW Harvey Milk St
SW Washington St
Oak/SW 1st
SW Front Ave
(Naito Pkwy)
MAX Light Rail
SW 3rd
SW Alder St

SW Oak
SW Pine
SW Ankeny St
W Burnside St
SW Oak St
SW Harvey Milk St
SW Washington St
SW Alder St
SW 6th Ave
Mall SW 5th
Pioneer Courthouse
Pioneer
Place
Mall SW 4th
SW 3rd

Pioneer
Courthouse
Pioneer
Square N
Pioneer Courthouse
Pioneer
Square S
Pioneer Mall

TriMet
Information
Center
Travel Portland

Library
SW 9th
Galleria
SW 10th
SW 9th Ave
SW Park Ave
SW Morrison St
SW 10th Ave
SW 11th Ave
SW 12th Ave
SW 13th Ave
SW 14th Ave
SW Yamhill St
SW Taylor St
SW Salmon St
SW Main St

MAX Light Rail

26 13 17 22 12 15 14 11 18 27 20 29 30 19 23 21 31 24 7

Downtown

Tom McCall
Waterfront Park

Yamhill
District

Portland
Spirit

Willamette River

Hawthorne
Bridge

Mill
Ends
Park 8

Salmon Street
Springs Fountain

For reviews see
- Top Sights   p30
- Sights   p40
- Eating   p42
- Drinking   p44
- Entertainment   p46
- Shopping   p47

200 m
0.1 miles

Lownsdale
Sq

Chapman
Sq

DOWNTOWN

Portland
Building

City Hall

Pettygrove
Park

Travelex

Oregon
Historical
Society

Portland
Art Museum

South
Park
Blocks

South
Park
Blocks

Portland
Streetcar

Portland
State
University

SW Clay St

SW Market St

SW Mill

SW Madison St
SW Madison
SW Jefferson St
SW Columbia St
SW Clay St
SW Market St
SW Mill St
SW Montgomery St
SW Harrison St

SW 1st Ave
SW 2nd Ave
SW 3rd Ave
SW 4th Ave
SW 5th Ave
SW Park Ave
SW Broadway
SW 10th Ave
SW 12th Ave

SW Salmon St
SW Main St
SW Madison St
SW Jefferson St
SW Columbia St
SW Clay St
SW Market St
SW Harrison St
SW Hall St

Sights

Salmon Street Springs Fountain
FOUNTAIN

1 MAP P38, F6

This photo-friendly fountain, on Salmon St near the river, cycles through computer-generated patterns. On hot days kids (and adults) take turns plunging through the jets. (1000 SW Naito Pkwy; ☒4, 10, 14, 15, 30)

Portland State University
LANDMARK

2 ◉ MAP P38, A7

This pretty campus is at the southwestern corner of downtown. There's a good farmers market here on Saturday, and several food carts around. (1825 SW Broadway)

South Park Blocks
PARK

3 ◉ MAP P38, B7

The South Park Blocks, a 12-block-long greenway that runs through much of downtown, are a fine, leafy refuge from downtown's bustle. They host a farmers market, occasional art shows, and are home to the Oregon Historical Society museum and the excellent Portland Art Museum. At the southern end of the South Park Blocks is Portland State University.

Portland Building
LANDMARK

4 ◉ MAP P38, D5

This controversial 15-story building (1982) was designed by Michael Graves and catapulted the postmodern architect to celebrity status. But the blocky, pastel-colored edifice has never been popular with the people who work inside it. The city found structural problems that led to massive reconstruction works that will be underway through the end of 2019; the pastel tiles will be replaced with terra-cotta ones. While it's currently covered, at least it's somewhat green: an eco-roof was installed in 2006.

Crouched over the main doors of the Portland Building is **Portlandia**. Made by sculptor Raymond Kaskey, the figure is, at just over 34ft, the second-largest hammered-copper statue in the US (after the Statue of Liberty). (1120 SW 5th Ave)

Oregon Historical Society
MUSEUM

5 ◉ MAP P38, B5

Along the tree-shaded South Park Blocks sits the state's primary history museum, which in 2019 unveiled a permanent 7000-sq-ft interactive exhibit that delves into Oregon's history, peoples and landscape. Stations include a canoe-building exercise, a walk-through covered-wagon replica and historical role-playing games. There are interesting sections on various immigrant groups, Native American tribes and the travails of the Oregon Trail. Temporary exhibits furnish the downstairs space. Check the website for free admission days. (☎503-222-1741; www.ohs.org; 1200

SW Park Ave; adult/child $10/5;
🕙10am-5pm Mon-Sat, noon-5pm Sun;
🚇Red, Blue)

Portland Art Museum MUSEUM

6 ◉ MAP P38, B5

Portland Art Museum's excellent exhibits include Native American carvings, Asian and American art, photography and English silver. The museum also houses the Whitsell Auditorium, a first-rate theater that frequently screens rare or international films and that is part of the Northwest Film Center and school. (📞503-226-2811; www. portlandartmuseum.org; 1219 SW Park Ave; adult/child $20/free; 🕙10am-5pm Tue, Wed, Sat & Sun, to 8pm Thu & Fri; 🚌6, 38, 45, 55, 58, 68, 92, 96, 🚊NS Line, A-Loop)

Pioneer Courthouse HISTORIC BUILDING

7 ◉ MAP P38, D4

Across 6th Ave from Pioneer Courthouse Square is the Pioneer Courthouse. Built in 1875, this was the legal center of 19th-century Portland. The courthouse's public areas, including the cupola, with views over downtown, are open to visitors. (www.pioneercourthouse. org; 700 SW 6th Ave; admission free; 🕙public areas 9am-4pm Mon-Fri; 🚇Red, Blue, Green)

Mill Ends Park PARK

8 ◉ MAP P38, F5

Having the largest park (Forest Park) within city limits perhaps isn't an oddity, but having the

Salmon Street Springs Fountain

Local Experiences

Hangouts For a breather between bouts of sightseeing and shopping, head to Pioneer Courthouse Square (p32). Grab a bite from one of the food carts here and settle onto the brick steps for grade-A people-watching, or bring a chess set and have a game.

Happy-hour grub There's no need to wait for dinner to experience some of Portland's best dining – most restaurants open up for happy hour before dinner service starts, and offer comprehensive menus that allow you to try house specialties in smaller portions for a fraction of the price.

Farmers-market food carts Development has resulted in the demise of the downtown's biggest food-cart pod, but you'll still find a few scattered throughout. Portland State University (p40) is home to a wonderful farmers market on Saturday, which has plenty of on-site food carts.

First Thursday Art Walk (www.firstthursdayportland.com) On the first Thursday of each month, many galleries extend their evening hours and show off new exhibits, often with wine and snacks. It's a bit of a mob scene but it's fun and fascinating.

smallest one might be. Mill Ends Park – located on a median strip – is a circle of green 24in in diameter (it's the reputed home of leprechauns). (SW Naito Pkwy & Taylor St)

Portland Spirit   CRUISE

9 ⊙ MAP P38, F6

Tour Portland from the water: these cruises offer sightseeing, historical narratives and/or meal combinations. (☎503-224-3900; www.portlandspirit.com; sightseeing/dinner cruise from $32/78; 🚋4, 10, 14, 15, 30)

Eating

Luc Lac   VIETNAMESE $

10 ✖ MAP P38, E5

This bustling Vietnamese kitchen draws downtown lunch crowds and late-night bar-hoppers with superbly executed classics like pho, vermicelli bowls and bahn mi. Count on queueing any time of day to score a seat in the swanky dining room, where pink paper parasols hang from the ceiling. Happy hour (4pm to 7pm) has a more relaxed vibe and small plates run just $3. (☎503-222-0047; www.luclackitchen.com; 835 SW 2nd Ave; mains $9-13; ⊙11am-2:30pm & 4pm-midnight Sun-Thu, 11am-2:30pm & 4pm-4am Fri & Sat)

Bullard   SOUTHERN US $$

Inside the Woodlark hotel (see 19 🚇 Map p38, C3) is this nod to chef Doug Adam's roots and chosen home, where the meat-centric menu is decidedly Texas-meets-Oregon. 'Supper' plates showcase the likes of 12-hour smoked Painted Hills beef ribs served with fresh flour tortillas, grilled rainbow trout with a black-eyed pea and celery salad, and a pork chop with heirloom hominy and local collard greens. (503-222-1670; www.bullardpdx. com; 813 SW Alder St; dinner mains $16-32; 11am-3pm & 5-10pm Mon-Thu, 11am-3pm & 5-11pm Fri, 10am-11pm Sat, 10am-10pm Sun)

Tasty n Alder FUSION $$

11 🗺 MAP P38, B2

Another of local restaurateur John Gorham's empire of Portland eateries, this downtown corner joint serves locally sourced, American interpretations of international dishes – duck breast grilled on a Spanish *plancha* or the awesome Korean *bibimbap* (rice, veggies and chili paste) served with bacon and eggs. Go for brunch on a weekday to avoid the crowds. (503-621-9251; www.tastynalder.com; 580 SW 12th Ave; mains $12-35; 9am-2pm & 5:30-10pm Sun-Thu, to 11pm Fri & Sat; 15, 51)

The Crown PIZZA $$

12 🗺 MAP P38, D2

Sister restaurant to chef Vitaly Paley's Imperial, this New York–style pizza joint inside Hotel Lucia is both a perfect lunch spot and a killer cocktail bar. Options include the signature Imperial pie, with fried chicken, pickles and ranch dressing, plus snacks, salads and slices. Large groups can go all-out with the 36in-long Al Metro, aka 'big-ass pizza' ($48). (503-228-7224; www.thecrownpdx.com; 410 SW Broadway; slices $4.75-6.75, pizzas $15-28; 11:30am-midnight Mon-Fri, from 3pm Sat & Sun)

Mother's Bistro AMERICAN $$

13 🗺 MAP P38, F2

Mother's is an upscale downtown spot beloved for its breakfast – try the salmon hash. For dinner, comfort food dishes include chicken and dumplings and meatloaf with gravy. The bright, cozy dining room features gilded accents and crystal chandeliers for a touch of class. You're guaranteed to wait in line on weekends. (503-464-1122; www. mothersbistro.com; 121 SW 3rd Ave; breakfast mains $9-17; 7am-2:30pm & 5:30-9pm Tue-Thu, to 10pm Fri, 8am-2:30pm & 5-10pm Sat, 8am-2:30pm Sun)

Kenny & Zuke's DELI $$

14 🗺 MAP P38, B2

The only place in the city for real Jewish deli food: bagels, pickled herring, homemade pickles and latkes (potato pancakes). But the real draw is the house pastrami, cut to order and gently sandwiched in one of the best Reubens you'll ever eat. It bustles for breakfast, too. (503-222-3354; www.kennyandzukes.com; 1038 SW Harvey Milk St; sandwiches $10-20; 7am-8pm Mon-Thu, to 9pm Fri, 8am-9pm Sat, 8am-8pm Sun)

Imperial
AMERICAN $$$

15 ✪ MAP P38, D2

Opened by long-adored Portland chef Vitaly Paley, the Imperial – attached to Hotel Lucia (www.hotellucia.com) – is huge in scale but fastidious and detail-oriented in approach. The kitchen is built around a massive wood-fire grill and rotisserie, and the menu exploits seasonal Northwest bounty – from rib eye and roasted chicken to grilled asparagus and ember-roasted potatoes. Great happy hour, too. (☏503-228-7222; www.imperialpdx.com; 410 SW Broadway; mains $11-45; ☉6:30am-10pm Mon-Thu, to 11pm Fri, 8am-11pm Sat, to 10pm Sun)

Higgins
FRENCH, NORTHWESTERN $$$

16 ✪ MAP P38, C6

In 1994 chef-owner Greg Higgins opened the doors to one of Portland's groundbreaking restaurants. These days, Higgins feels more classically elegant than cutting edge, but it still features French-inspired dishes like duck confit with brandied cherries, using seasonal Northwest ingredients. The beer list is among the best in town; ask for pairing suggestions for any course. (☏503-222-9070; www.higginsportland.com; 1239 SW Broadway; mains $26-47; ☉11:30am-midnight Mon-Fri, from 5pm Sat & Sun)

Little Bird
FRENCH $$$

17 ✪ MAP P38, D2

Sister restaurant to lower E Burnside's renowned Le Pigeon (p111) is this quaint French bistro. Folks swoon over the *poulet et porc* and chicken-fried trout; don't miss the pricey but sublime desserts ($11 to $15). It also serves a double-brie burger with spiced ketchup, one of Portland's best ($16). (☏503-688-5952; www.littlebirdbistro.com; 215 SW 6th Ave; mains $16-39; ☉11:30am-11pm Mon-Fri, from 5pm Sat & Sun)

Jake's Famous Crawfish
SEAFOOD $$$

18 ✪ MAP P38, B2

Saunter into this classic joint, reservation in hand. You'll need it – some of Portland's best seafood can be found here within an elegant old-time atmosphere. The oysters are divine, the crab cakes a revelation and the seafood-stuffed Chinook salmon your ticket to heaven. Come at happy hour for more affordable treats. (☏503-226-1419; www.jakesfamouscrawfish.com; 401 SW 12th Ave; mains $22-47; ☉11:30am-10pm Mon-Thu, to 11pm Fri & Sat, 10am-10pm Sun)

Drinking

Abigail Hall
COCKTAIL BAR

19 ✪ MAP P38, C3

Just beyond the lobby of the Woodlark hotel (https://woodlarkhotel.

com) is Abigail Hall, the hotel bar named after an Oregon suffragette and the women's reception hall that once inhabited the historic space. Retro floral wallpaper, stiff-backed banquettes and plaid wingback chairs deliver a punch of granny chic, while cocktails with names like 'Born on the Bayeux' and 'Summer in Aberdeen' conjure foregone times.

There's a good bar menu that includes prawn cocktails, fried chicken fingers, steak bites and a Dungeness crab roll. (www.abigailhallpdx.com; 813 SW Alder St; ⊙3pm-late)

Courier Coffee Roasters
COFFEE

20 MAP P38, C1

Courier is a small-batch roaster with friendly baristas and a great macchiato. Exceptional pastries, too. Go for an iced drink on a hot day. It delivers its roasted beans by cargo bicycle, among other sustainable practices. (📱503-545-6444; www.couriercoffeeroasters.com; 923 SW Oak St; ⊙7am-6pm Mon-Fri, 9am-5pm Sat & Sun; 📶)

Departure Lounge
BAR

21 MAP P38, D4

This rooftop restaurant-bar, atop the 15th floor of the Nines hotel (www.thenines.com), fills a deep downtown void: a cool bar with unforgettable views of Portland. The vibe is distinctly 'spaceship LA,' with mod couches and sleek

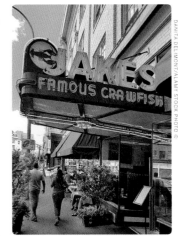
Jake's Famous Crawfish

lighting. Hit happy hour from 4pm to 6pm (or late night) for select drinks and appetizers. (📱503-802-5370; www.departureportland.com; 525 SW Morrison St; ⊙4-11pm Sun-Thu, to midnight Fri & Sat; 🚌1, 8, 12, 94, 🚊Green, Yellow, Blue, Red)

Bailey's Taproom
BREWERY

22 MAP P38, D2

This popular, non-intimidating place has a rotating selection of 26 eclectic beers and ciders from Oregon and beyond. It's a fun place to try something new – the digital menu board tells you about the beers, and how much of each is left. No food served, but you can bring stuff in from outside. (📱503-295-1004; www.baileystaproom.com; 213 SW Broadway; ⊙noon-midnight)

The Specials perform at the Crystal Ballroom

Public Domain Coffee

COFFEE

23 MAP P38, C3

A swanky downtown outlet with shiny high-end espresso machines, owned by long-time indie roasters Coffee Bean International. (☎503-243-6374; www.publicdomaincoffee.com; 603 SW Broadway; ⏱6am-5pm; 📶)

Entertainment

Flicks on the Bricks

CINEMA

24 ⭐ MAP P38, D4

On certain Fridays in summer, the Pioneer Courthouse Square becomes a huge outdoor cinema showing free movies on a big screen. Bring your own chairs or take a seat on the brick steps. (www.thesquarepdx.org/events; ⏱7pm Fri Jul & Aug; 🚇Red, Blue Green)

Keller Auditorium

PERFORMING ARTS

25 ⭐ MAP P38, D7

Built in 1917 and formerly known as the Civic Auditorium, Keller hosts a wide range of performers, from big-name musicians (Sturgill Simpson) to the Portland Opera (www.portlandopera.org) and the Oregon Ballet Theatre (www.obt.org), along with some Broadway productions. (☎503-248-4335; www.portland5.com; 222 SW Clay St; 🚌38, 45, 55, 92, 96)

Dante's

LIVE MUSIC

26 ⭐ MAP P38, F1

This steamy red bar books burlesque and cabaret shows along with national and regional touring bands (including the Murder City Devils, the Supersuckers and the Sugarhill Gang). Drop in on Sunday night for the eclectic Sinferno Cabaret, and on Monday night for Karaoke from Hell. (☎tickets 866-777-8932; www.danteslive.com; 350 W Burnside St)

Crystal Ballroom

LIVE MUSIC

27 ⭐ MAP P38, A1

This large, historic ballroom has hosted some major acts, including James Brown and Marvin Gaye in the early '60s, and Devendra Banhart and Two Door Cinema

Club today. The bouncy, 'floating' dance floor makes dancing almost effortless. (📞503-225-0047; www.crystalballroompdx.com; 1332 W Burnside St; 🚍20)

Arlene Schnitzer Concert Hall

CLASSICAL MUSIC

28 ⭐ MAP P38, C5

This beautiful, if not acoustically brilliant, downtown venue, built in 1928, hosts a wide range of shows, lectures, concerts and other performances. (📞503-248-4335; www.portland5.com; 1037 SW Broadway; 🚍10, 14, 15, 35, 36, 44, 54, 56)

Shopping

Tender Loving Empire

GIFTS & SOUVENIRS

29 🔒 MAP P38, C2

This small gift shop is so Portland it hurts: in addition to selling adorable handmade goods by local 'makers,' it's also an independent record label, with in-store listening station, plus a tiny art gallery. Can you guess it's really into promoting local art and creativity? (📞503-243-5859; www.tenderlovingempire.com; 412 SW 10th Ave; 🕙10:30am-6:30pm)

Finnegan's Toys & Gifts

TOYS

30 🔒 MAP P38, C3

Crammed with toys of all kinds, this chaotic kids' store is fun to explore. (📞503-221-0306; www.finnegantoys.

Big Brands, No Sales Tax

The downtown area is where you'll find a majority of Portland's outposts for big-name brands, primarily around Pioneer Place Mall and near Pioneer Courthouse Square. There are lots of local boutiques and concept stores in the area as well, particularly northwest of Pioneer Courthouse Square, running up to W Burnside St. And remember, there's no sales tax in Oregon so everything is likely cheaper than you'll find at home.

com; 820 SW Washington St; 🕙11am-6pm Mon-Fri, from 10am Sat, 11am-5pm Sun)

Pioneer Place

MALL

31 🔒 MAP P38, D4

A big, semi-upscale shopping center downtown, Pioneer Place has a food court in the basement and is handy to public transit. (📞503-228-5800; www.pioneerplace.com; 700 SW 5th Ave; 🕙10am-8pm Mon-Sat, 11am-6pm Sun)

Top Sight 📷
Washington Park

Tame and well-tended Washington Park contains several attractions within its 410 green acres. The International Rose Test Garden is the centerpiece of Portland's famous rose blooms. Further uphill is the Japanese Garden, another oasis of tranquility. If you have kids, the Oregon Zoo and Portland Children's Museum should be on your docket.

www.washington
parkpdx.org

🚻

🚌 63, 🚊 Blue, Red
🚊 Washington Park

Gardens Galore

Often called the most authentic Japanese garden outside Japan, the **Japanese Garden** (☎503-223-1321; www.japanesegarden.org; 611 SW Kingston Ave; adult/child $17/11.50; ☺noon-7pm Mon, 10am-7pm Tue-Sun mid-Mar–Sep, to 4pm Oct–mid-Mar) is a sanctuary. It was conceived as a symbol of post-WWII healing between the US and Japan when Portland and Sapporo became sister cities in 1959.

Meanwhile, the **International Rose Test Garden** (pictured; www.waparkrosefriends.org; 400 SW Kingston Ave; admission free; ☺7:30am-9pm) practically gave Portland its 'Rose City' nickname. It sprawls across 4.5 acres of lawns, fountains and flowerbeds, and on a clear day you can catch peeks of downtown and Mt Hood. Over 700 rose varieties grow here; from April to September the scent is intoxicating.

Hoyt Arboretum

Twelve miles of trails wind through this 189-acre ridge-top **garden** (☎503-865-8733; www.hoytarboretum.org; 4000 Fairview Blvd; admission free; ☺trails 5am-10pm, visitor center 9am-4pm Mon-Fri, from 10am Sat & Sun) above the city zoo. It's home to over 6000 native and exotic plants and trees representing 1100 different species, and it offers easy walks any time of year.

Washington Park for Kids

The well-run **Oregon Zoo** (☎503-226-1561; www.oregonzoo.org; 4001 SW Canyon Rd; adult/child $18/13; ☺9:30am-6pm Jun-Aug, to 4pm Sep-May; ♦) has many impressive exhibits. Enclosures are spacious and semi-natural. Concerts take place on the zoo's lawns in summer.

On rainy days, families can seek solace at the **Portland Children's Museum** (☎503-233-6500; www.portlandcm.org; 4015 SW Canyon Rd; $11, 2nd Sunday of each month 9am-noon $3; ☺9am-5pm; ♦), a great place to keep kids busy with interesting learning activities and exhibits.

★ **Top Tips**

○ Complimentary Japanese Garden tours typically take place at 2pm and 4pm from May 1 through Labor Day, and at noon from September 4 through April 30. Call to confirm.

○ From June to late September, volunteers lead Rose Garden tours daily, starting from the Rose Garden Store at 1pm (call ahead to confirm).

✗ **Take a Break**

The Japanese Garden's **Umami Cafe** serves traditional Japanese tea sets served with sweets or savory dishes like fried rice bowls.

★ **Getting There**

Light Rail Red and Blue lines.

Bus Routes 15 and 20.

Shuttle The Explore Washington Park Shuttle runs May to October and stops at the park's major attractions.

Explore

Old Town Chinatown

The core of rambunctious 1890s Portland, once-seedy Old Town was the lurking ground of unsavory characters. Now it's home to historic buildings, Waterfront Park, the Saturday Market and good nightlife.

Old Town is generally lumped together with historic Chinatown – no longer the heart of the Chinese community, but home to the ornate Chinatown Gateway and the Lan Su Chinese Garden.

The Short List

o **Lan Su Chinese Garden (p52)** *Admiring the traditional architecture and landscaped haven.*

o **Saturday Market (p54)** *Browsing creations in the country's largest and longest-running open-art arts-and-crafts market.*

o **Japanese American Historical Plaza (p60)** *Reflecting on the Pacific Northwest's Japanese-American residents who were forced into internment camps during WWII.*

o **Darcelle XV (p64)** *Reveling in the big-wig, cabaret splendor, all led by the city's octogenarian drag queen.*

o **Voodoo Doughnut (p61)** *Queuing for creative doughnuts – and taking them to go in a big pink box.*

Getting There & Around

🚆 The Red and Blue MAX light-rail lines run along 1st Ave on the eastern side of the district; the Yellow and Green lines run along NW 6th Ave on the western side.

🚌 Routes 1, 4, 5, 8, 10, 16, 33, 40 and 77 serve the area.

Neighborhood Map on p58

Lan Su Chinese Garden (p52) ARTYOORAN/SHUTTERSTOCK ©

Top Sight 📷
Lan Su Chinese Garden

A tranquil oasis set in the bustle of the city, Lan Su Chinese Garden is a wonderful place to reflect among nature and learn about Chinese culture. Spanning 40,000 sq ft, the authentic Ming Dynasty–style space features koi ponds, seasonal foliage and traditional architecture. Cultural events and demonstrations by community organizations and local experts take place year-round.

◉ MAP P58, C2

📞 503-228-8131

www.lansugarden.org

239 NW Everett St

adult/student $11/8

🕐 10am-7pm mid-May–mid-Oct, shorter hours rest of year

🚌 8, 77, 🚈 Blue, Red

Architecture & Landscape

As one of the most traditional Chinese gardens in the US, Lan Su's grounds feature pavilions, bridges, open colonnades, covered walkways, ponds and meticulously tended foliage.

In 1988 Suzhou, China, was designated a sister city of Portland, fueling ambitions for creating a traditional Chinese garden in the city. More than a decade later, in 1999, 65 artisans from Suzhou began constructing the walled botanical complex on a plot of land donated by the Northwest Natural Gas Company.

Native Chinese flora that shifts with the seasons is found throughout the garden's verdant landscape. Horticulture enthusiasts can learn more about Lan Su's landscape during the 45-minute 'plant walk' guided tour that takes place every Tuesday at 2pm.

Art

In the garden pavilions, Lan Su showcases classic and contemporary works by artists from the Pacific Northwest and beyond. Visitors can also partake in a range of demonstrations on calligraphy, poetry and brush and silk painting from classically trained artists and scholars.

Culture

Everything at Lan Su represents harmony, beauty and a reverence for tradition – even its name, which is a derivation of both Portland ('Lan') and Suzhou ('Su'). 'Lan' is the Chinese word for 'orchid', and 'su' is the word for 'arise' or 'awaken', making Lan Su's poetic appellation 'garden of awakening orchids'.

Lan Su serves as a beacon of Chinese culture and community in Portland. In partnership with more than 50 local organizations, demonstrations, lessons and other educational events take place almost every day and are typically included with the price of admission.

★ Top Tips

◦ Horticulture enthusiasts should check out Lan Su's 'Bloom Guide,' which features the top 16 varieties of flora visible in the garden during each season. Pick up a copy at the admission desk, or download it from the website.

◦ Public tours begin in the Courtyard of Tranquility a few times per day, and are included with admission. Check the website for exact days and times.

✕ Take a Break

The garden has a two-story **teahouse**, located in the Tower of Cosmic Reflections. Traditional tea presentations are offered, along with pastries, snacks, and light dishes like noodle bowls, dumplings, buns and soups.

Otherwise, just around the corner from the garden, you'll find Little Taco & Tequila (p61) serving up great street tacos, margaritas and more.

Top Sight 📷
Saturday Market

Established in 1974, Portland's Saturday Market is the longest-running open-air craft market in the US. From March through Christmas Eve, hundreds of hometown vendors hawk everything under the sun on Saturdays and Sundays. It's a one-stop shop for picking up handcrafted creations, checking out musical performances and sampling international food-cart fare.

◎ MAP P58, F5

☏ 503-222-6072

www.portland
saturdaymarket.com

2 SW Naito Pkwy

🕑 10am-5pm Sat, 11am-4:30pm Sun Mar-Dec

🚌 12, 16, 19, 20

🚇 Red, Blue

Market History

Artists Sheri Teasdale and Andrea Scharf founded the market as a mutual benefit corporation that would require vendors to contribute to costs and administration, but keep all the profits earned from selling their wares. They also determined that everything at the market must be handmade by the seller.

Today, more than 750,000 visit each year, generating some $12 million in gross sales annually.

What to Look For

If you can dream it, you can probably find it at this market. With more than 350 local artisans and craftspeople selling their creations here, variety is the word.

Check out the booths run by everyone from woodworkers and jewelry-makers to folks making dried flowers cast in crystal or blown-glass bird feeders.

It's a great place to score gifts around Christmas too. During the final week of the market, the **Festival of the Last Minute** (11am to 5pm Monday to Friday, 10am to 5pm Saturday, 11am to 3:30pm Sunday) is open every day.

Shop to the Beat

While people-watching at the market makes for great entertainment, you'll also catch local musicians playing original music on the 'Main Stage' next to the Bill Naito Legacy Fountain in Tom McCall Waterfront Park. Genres range from acoustic folk and swing to blues and alternative rock. The tempos are kept upbeat and lively, just like the market's atmosphere.

For mini market-goers, there's a 'Kids' Korner' that has activities such as puppet shows and hands-on craft activities, led by different organizations like the Portland's Children Museum.

★ Top Tips

○ Each year, a different artist is commissioned to design the cover of the market's annual souvenir booklet, which includes a map. View it online at www.psmsouvenirbooklet.com, or email info@saturdaymarket.org to receive a printed copy in the mail.

○ If you make a $25 purchase at the market, you'll receive a free TriMet ticket or up to two hours of parking validation at any of the city's Smart Park garages.

✕ Take a Break

The market's **International Food Court** has everything from Nepalese to Guatemalan. Grab a bite and keep wandering.

If you need to take a load off, Pine Street Market (p62) is a couple of blocks away.

Walking Tour

Wandering Old Town Chinatown

This walk takes you through some of Portland's rich Asian history and influence as well as to some quirky, modern and off-the-tourist radar stops. Along the way you'll get to stroll the banks of the lovely Willamette River, shop, shoot pinball, re-fuel with coffee and eat tacos for a very Portland-y adventure.

Walk Facts

Start New Market Theater (🚉 Blue)

End Lan Su Chinese Garden (🚌 8, 4; 🚉 Blue)

Length 1 mile; three hours

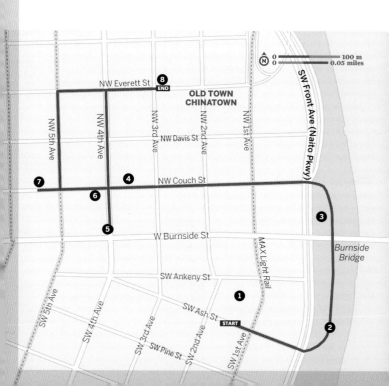

❶ Nostalgic architecture

Kick off your stroll at the **New Market Theater** (p60), where you can admire circa 1872 details such as the arches that face SW 1st Ave. Adding to the nostalgic architecture is the **Skidmore Fountain** (p60), just across the street at the corner of SW 1st Ave and SW Ankeny St.

❷ Market action

If you're here on a weekend, you'll be right in the middle of the **Saturday Market** (p54) action, which spreads all the way to the riverside **Tom McCall Waterfront Park** (p30).

❸ Historic plaza's cherry trees

Located within the park, just north of the Burnside Bridge, is the **Japanese American Historical Plaza** (p60), where one hundred cherry trees line the river.

❹ Handmade goodies

From there, cross over Naito Pkwy to NW Couch St. Continue three blocks to **Kiriko Made** (p64). Browse the handmade clothing and home goods that are all made with vintage Japanese textiles and techniques.

❺ Gateway to Chinatown

Next, walk a block south down NW 4th Ave till you see the **Chinatown Gateway** (p60). After admiring its ornate details, head to **Tope** (p62) on the Hoxton Hotel's rooftop for a drink with a wonderful view.

❻ Caffeine & sneakers & bags, oh my!

Head back up NW 4th Ave and take a left on Couch St. Pop into **Deadstock Coffee** (p63), a laid-back shop dedicated to sneaker culture. Next door, you can watch beautiful leather bags and accessories come to life at family-run **Orox Leather Goods** (p64) – and shop their wares.

❼ Old-skool video games

Continue another block west on Couch St to NW 5th Ave and check out **Ground Kontrol Classic Arcade** (p63) for a round of pinball or old-school video games like Pac-Man. If that whets your appetite you can load up on Mexican street food at nearby **Little Taco & Tequila** (p61).

❽ Lan Su tranquility

Finish the walk at the **Lan Su Chinese Garden** (p52), located catty-corner at the end of the block on NW Everett St. It's a tranquil place to digest as you admire the traditional Chinese architecture and landscaping – tai chi and kung fu classes are also regularly scheduled.

Old Town Chinatown

SW Front Ave (Naito Pkwy)

Tom McCall
Waterfront
Park

Japanese
American
Historical
Plaza 2

Old Town
Chinatown

NW 1st Ave

OLD TOWN
CHINATOWN

NW 2nd Ave

Lan Su
Chinese
Garden

15

1 Shanghai
Tunnels
18

NW 3rd Ave

19

W Burnside St

7

NW Everett St

NW Davis St

NW Flanders St

21

20

NW Couch St

Chinatown
5 Gateway

NW 4th Ave

12

14 24
22

NW Couch

NW 5th Ave

13 23

NW Davis

NW 6th Ave

16

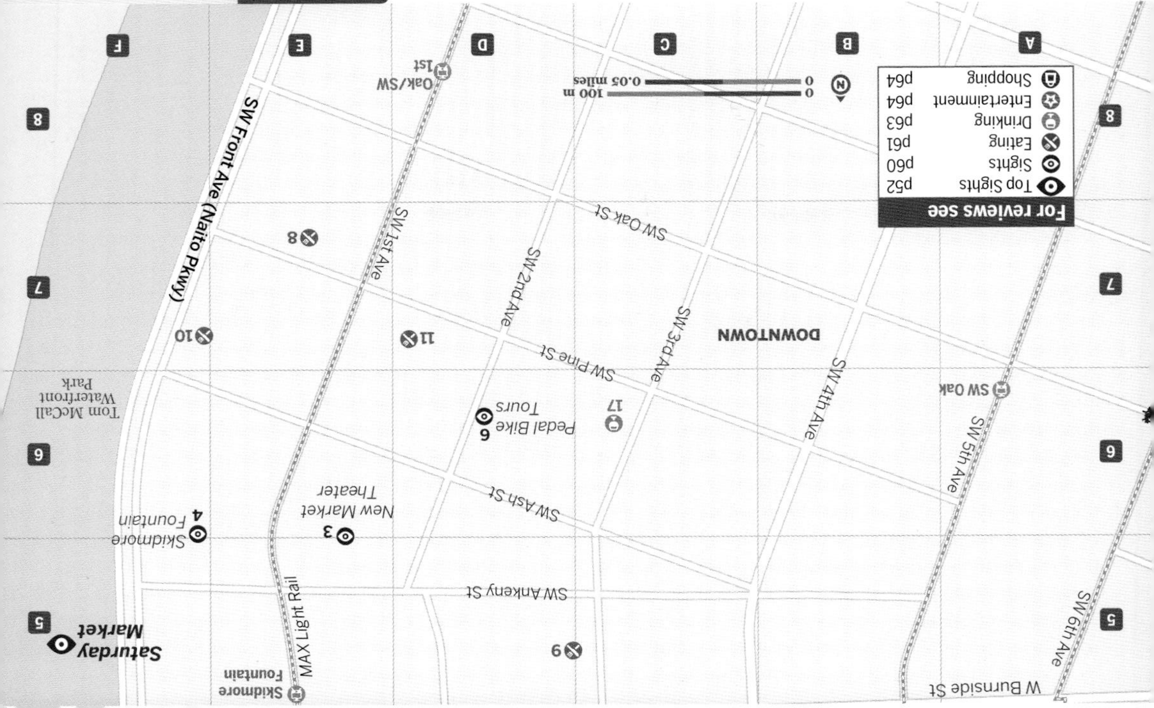

Old Town Chinatown

Saturday Market ⓞ 5

Skidmore Fountain ⓞ 4

Skidmore Fountain

MAX Light Rail

New Market Theater ⓞ 3

Tom McCall Waterfront Park

SW Front Ave (Naito Pkwy)

❌ 10

❌ 8

❌ 11

SW 1st Ave

Oak/SW 1st

SW Ankeny St

❌ 9

SW Ash St

Pedal Bike Tours ⓞ 6

ⓘ 17

SW 2nd Ave

SW Pine St

SW 3rd Ave

SW Oak St

DOWNTOWN

SW 4th Ave

100 m
0.05 miles

SW 5th Ave

SW Oak

Ⓝ

W Burnside St

SW 5th Ave

SW 6th Ave

For reviews see
ⓞ Top Sights	p52
ⓞ Sights	p60
❌ Eating	p61
🍷 Drinking	p63
🎭 Entertainment	p64
🛍 Shopping	p64

5

6

7

8

F

E

D

C

B

A

Sights

Shanghai Tunnels
HISTORIC SITE

1 ◉ MAP P58, C3

Downtown Portland's basements were once connected by tunnels running beneath the streets and down to riverside docks. While they were built for shipping and flood control, rumors persist that they were also used to transport unconscious men to be sold to unscrupulous ship's captains. Most of the tunnels have long been sealed, but remnants can be visited by tour. (☎503-622-4798; 120 NW 3rd Ave; adult/child $13/8; ☐12, 19, 20, ☒Blue, Red)

Japanese American Historical Plaza
MEMORIAL

2 ◉ MAP P58, F4

North of the Burnside Bridge, the Japanese American Historical Plaza is a memorial to Japanese Americans who were sent to internment camps by the US government during WWII. Artwork in the memorial garden depicts the story of the Pacific Northwest's Japanese residents. A bronze and stone sculpture named *Songs of Innocence, Songs of Experience* by artist Jim Gion forms the gateway to the plaza. (Tom McCall Waterfront Park)

New Market Theater
LANDMARK

3 ◉ MAP P58, E6

This landmark was built in 1872 and is notable for the cast iron arches facing SW 1st Ave, all that are left of its northern wing. (50 SW 2nd Ave; ☒Blue)

Skidmore Fountain
FOUNTAIN

4 ◉ MAP P58, F6

Victorian-era architecture and the attractive Skidmore Fountain give the area beneath the Burnside Bridge some nostalgic flair. Dedicated in 1888, the National Historic Landmark site is Portland's oldest piece of public art.

Chinatown Gateway
GATE

5 ◉ MAP P58, B4

Though it was once the second-largest Chinatown in the US, don't expect flashbacks of Shanghai in Portland's Chinese quarter these days – most of its former residents and businesses have moved to outer Southeast neighborhoods. Still, the deceptively impressive pagoda-style Chinatown Gateway remains a beloved local landmark and a symbol of the city's Chinese heritage. (☐20)

Pedal Bike Tours
CYCLING

6 ◉ MAP P58, D6

Offers all sorts of themes – history, doughnuts, beer – plus day trips to the Columbia Gorge. The three-hour 'bike & boat' package includes a historic bike tour of downtown and a sightseeing cruise with Portland Spirit (p42). (☎503-243-2453; www.pedalbiketours.com; 133 SW 2nd Ave; tours from $49; ⊘10am-6pm; ☐15, 16, 51, ☒Blue, Red)

Eating

Little Taco & Tequila

MEXICAN $

7 MAP P58, C2

For superbly executed street tacos, tamale and *sopes,* try this taqueria in Old Town. Open late on weekends, it pours more than 75 types of tequila, which you can order in flights. Top-notch specialty margaritas are concocted with house-made syrups – take your pick from blueberry hibiscus mint, serrano sage cucumber, papaya rose hip, rosemary watermelon, chocolate sumac or blood orange saffron. (📞503-274-8226; www.littlett.com; 215 NW 3rd Ave; tacos $3.50-4; ⏲11am-10pm Sun-Thu, to 3am Fri & Sat)

Kalé

JAPANESE CURRY $

8 MAP P58, E7

Kalé does one thing with minimal variation – and does it well. Its homestyle Japanese curry, composed of onions, carrots, garlic, celery and tomatoes, is cooked for two days before finally being served alongside rice and adorned with chicken, beef or veggies. The dining room features bright lights, cheery red accents and a mural of abstract veggies on the wall. (📞503-206-4114; www.kalepdx.com; 50 SW Pine St; curries $9-12; ⏲11am-8pm Mon-Thu, to 9pm Fri & Sat)

Voodoo Doughnut

DESSERTS $

9 MAP P58, D5

There's nothing quite like this standing-room-only hole-in-the-wall

Songs of Innocence, Songs of Experience by Jim Gion

Weekend Street Party

On weekend nights, several blocks of Old Town China-town closes off to vehicular traffic and the area becomes a pedestrians-only zone with the party spilling out into the streets. If you've come to Portland for alcohol-fueled revelry on the dance floor, this is where you'll find it.

(pun intended) spot. It bakes creative, sickly-sweet treats – go for the surprisingly good bacon-maple bar or the 'cock 'n balls' (shaped like a...well, yes). Part of the fun is standing in line with everyone else, and then carrying around that distinctive pink box so people know where you've been. (☏503-241-4704; www.voodoodoughnut.com; 22 SW 3rd Ave; doughnuts from $2; ⊙24hr)

LeChon SOUTH AMERICAN $$

10 MAP P58, F7

This under-the-radar eatery on the waterfront specializes in South American fare. Dishes from Argentina, Chile, Patagonia and Peru include pork *anticucho* (grilled heart), *lomo saltado* (sirloin strips with rice and fries), empanadas and ceviche. If you're after an extravaganza, try the *asado* (grilled meat) main – flank steak, lamb T-bone,

sweetbreads and smoked sausages will stuff you to the gills. (☏503-219-9000; www.lechonpdx.com; 113 SW Naito Pkwy; mains $12-28; ⊙11am-2pm & 4:30-10pm Mon-Thu, to 11pm Fri, 3-11pm Sat, 3-10pm Sun)

Pine Street Market AMERICAN $$

11 MAP P58, D7

An indoor food hall in the historic Baggage and Carriage Building downtown, Pine Street Market collects eight buzz-worthy restaurants and cafes around a central dining area, including outlets from the minds behind Salt & Straw (ice cream) and Olympia Provisions (p76). (www.pinestreetpdx.com; 126 SW 2nd Ave; prices vary; ⊙9am-11pm)

Tope MEXICAN $$

12 MAP P58, B4

This taqueria and bar on the rooftop of the Hoxton hotel stuns with floor-to-ceiling white tiles, hanging plants, warm wood furnishings and gold accents. Street tacos include *lengua* (tongue), fried rock fish, beef cheek *adobo*, spicy lamb sausage and roasted cauliflower, though the execution of some left us wanting. While you can find better tacos elsewhere, views from here can't be beat. (☏503-770-0500; www.thehoxton.com; 15 NW 4th Ave; tacos $4-6, snacks $2-19; ⊙4-10pm Sun & Mon, to 11pm Tue-Thu, to midnight Fri & Sat; 🚌20)

Drinking

Ground Kontrol Classic Arcade

BAR

13 MAP P58, A3

Remember Galaga? You can still play it at this awesome video arcade for adults, along with plenty of other vintage arcade games and pinball machines. A recent expansion into the building next door doubled the venue's size. There's a basic bar food menu as well as beer, wine and cocktails. Check online for 'free play' nights and other events. (503-796-9364; www.groundkontrol.com; 115 NW 5th Ave; games 25-50¢; noon-2:30am; 20, Green, Orange, Yellow)

Deadstock Coffee

COFFEE

14 MAP P58, B4

Deadstock's ethos that 'coffee should be dope' comes through in its signature concoctions and blends, such as the LeBronald Palmer (a mix of iced coffee, sweet tea and lemonade) and Fresh Prince (Ethiopian light-roast beans). Owner Ian Williams once worked his way from janitor to shoe designer at Nike HQ, and it's the world's only coffee shop dedicated to sneaker culture. (971-220-8727; www.deadstockcoffee.com; 408 NW Couch St; 7:30am-5pm Mon-Fri, 9am-6pm Sat, 10am-4pm Sun)

CC Slaughters

LGBT+

15 MAP P58, D2

This popular, long-running night-club boasts a big, loud dance floor and good DJs. When you tire of shaking your bootie, head into the relaxed Rainbow Room lounge. There's a Sunday-night drag show and fun themed nights. (503-248-9135; www.ccslaughterspdx.com; 219 NW Davis St; 3pm-2:30am)

Silverado

GAY

16 MAP P58, A4

Expect almost nightly stripper shows at this club catering to men. It's a mixed crowd with cheap drinks, potential groping and muscled dancers – bring plenty of dollar bills and count on a wild time. If you need a breather, there's an outdoor terrace and lounge with a pool table and video poker, thanks to a recent move to a bigger space. (503-224-4493; www.silveradopdx.com; 610 NW Couch St; 9pm-2:30am)

Stumptown Coffee Roasters – Downtown

COFFEE

17 MAP P58, C6

The downtown location of the famous Portland coffee roasting empire is the most spacious and has art shows that change monthly. (www.stumptowncoffee.com; 128 SW 3rd Ave; 6am-7pm Mon-Fri, 7am-7pm Sat & Sun;)

Sporty Shopping

In the hometown of Nike, you can bet this city is filled with lovers of athletic apparel. Old Town Chinatown is the best place in town to find local retailers who specialize in streetwear, both new and vintage.

Hobo's   GAY

18 🚇 MAP P58, C3

Past the old historic storefront here is a classy gay-centric restaurant and piano bar. It's a quiet, relaxed place and good for a romantic dinner or drink; for some activity, head to the pool tables in back. Live music starts at 7pm from Thursday to Sunday. (📞503-224-3285; www.hobospdx.com; 120 NW 3rd Ave; ⏰4pm-2:30am Sun-Fri, from 3pm Sat)

Entertainment

Darcelle XV   CABARET

19 ⭐ MAP P58, C2

This is Portland's Vegas-style cabaret show, featuring glitzy drag queens in big wigs, fake jewelry and overstuffed bras. Musical performances are spiced with corny comedy, while hapless audience members are picked out and teased. Male strippers perform at midnight on Friday and Saturday. Reservations aren't required, but recommended for shows Wednesday through Saturday. (📞503-222-5338; www.darcellexv.com; 208 NW 3rd Ave; $20; ⏰8pm Wed-Sat, 10:30pm Fri & Sat)

Shopping

Kiriko Made   CLOTHING

20 🔒 MAP P58, C3

For truly one-of-a-kind gifts that also tick the sustainable box, turn to this atelier and boutique that creates clothing, accessories and home goods from vintage Japanese textiles. The owner uses centuries-old traditional dyeing and stitching techniques to reimagine garments like kimonos, dresses, shirts and aprons in a modern aesthetic. (📞503-222-0335; https://kirikomade.com; 325 NW Couch St; ⏰10am-6pm Mon-Fri, from noon Sat & Sun)

Laundry   VINTAGE

21 🔒 MAP P58, C3

In a city that's chock-full of great secondhand shopping, Laundry offers something unique, specializing in premium vintage streetwear and sports apparel. You can score old-school Starter jackets, band tees, player jerseys and snap-back caps, plus all the throwback Polo, Tommy Hilfiger and Nautica gear that your '90s self once desired. (www.laundrypdx.com; 140 NW 4th Ave; ⏰11am-6pm Mon-Sat, to 5pm Sun)

Orox Leather Goods   FASHION & ACCESSORIES

22 🔒 MAP P58, B4

A love for leather craft spans four generations at family-owned and operated Orox. Their roots are in

LORI BUTCHER/SHUTTERSTOCK ©

Voodoo Doughnut (p61)

Oaxaca, but everything is hand-made right in the Old Town Chinatown store, which is half showroom and half production workshop. Take in the aroma of raw leather and sewing machine oil as you browse beautiful bags, wallets, shoes, belts and hats. (✆503-954-2593; www.oroxleather.com; 450 NW Couch St; ⊗10am-5pm Mon-Sat)

Compound Gallery
CONCEPT STORE

23 🔒 MAP P58, A3

Peddling trendy threads, sneakers, backpacks and collectable toys since 2002, this bi-level retailer and gallery is where streetwear hype and Japanese pop-art culture collide. Local and underground designers are showcased alongside big-name brands; it has a boutique Nike account, so you're likely to score coveted, hard-to-find kicks here. Regular community events are hosted in the space. (✆503-796-2733; www.compoundgallery.com; 107 NW 5th & Couch St; ⊗11am-7pm Mon-Thu, to 8pm Sat, noon-6pm Sun)

Floating World Comics
BOOKS

24 🔒 MAP P58, B4

An excellent comic bookstore in Old Town, with a vast but well-curated selection ranging from superhero to literary. (✆503-241-0227; www.floatingworldcomics.com; 400 NW Couch St; ⊗11am-7pm)

Explore ⊕

Northwest & the Pearl District

Northwest Portland encompasses three distinct neighborhoods all connected by walkable streets. Nob Hill's arts-and-crafts-style storefronts house restaurants and shops amid Victorian homes. Industrial Slabtown is up-and-coming with new high-rise residences, while the once-industrial Pearl District is characterized by its cobblestone streets, old loading docks and boutiques and is now one of the state's chicest neighborhoods.

The Short List

○ **Powell's City of Books (p68)** *Losing yourself to a whole city block of books at the nation's largest independent bookstore.*

○ **Cinema 21 (p71)** *Settling into an independent or foreign flick at Portland's top art-house cinema.*

○ **Barista (p77)** *Stopping for coffee at one of the city's best shops, boasting award-winning baristas.*

○ **Pearl District shopping (p78)** *Browsing blocks of beloved international brands to homegrown hits such as MadeHere PDX, all tax-free.*

○ **Breweries (p77)** *Sipping craft brews at buzzing tap houses like Breakside Brewery.*

Getting There & Around

🚋 All streetcar lines (A Loop, B Loop and NS Line) serve the Pearl District; the NS Line runs from the South Waterfront in the West Hills to NW 23rd St in Nob Hill.

🚌 Route 15 runs from Southeast Portland to Nob Hill, via downtown. Route 20 runs along Burnside St from Southeast Portland to Nob Hill.

Neighborhood Map on p72

Pearl District HEMIS/ALAMY STOCK PHOTO ©

Top Sight 📷
Powell's City of Books

Powell's City of Books is a Portland institution. Occupying five floors and spanning an entire city block, the iconic retailer is the largest independent bookstore in the country. Its nine color-coded rooms house millions of books on every subject imaginable, and with throngs of individuals wandering the stacks each day, it's one of the best places in Portland for people-watching.

◉ MAP P72, G6

📞 800-878-7323

www.powells.com

1005 W Burnside St

🕘 9am-11pm

🚌 20

A Family Affair

Powell's took root in Chicago, where Michael Powell opened his first bookstore in 1970. Michael's father, Walter – a retired painting contractor – spent the summer of 1971 working in the Chicago store. He enjoyed it so much that he opened his own used bookstore upon returning home to Portland.

Walter's operation soon outgrew the original location. Around the time that Michael left Chicago to join Walter in Portland, with his wife and infant daughter, Emily, in tow, the Powells moved things over to the store's current location, a former old car dealership on NW Burnside St.

In 2010 Michael's daughter, Emily, took over operations for Powell's. She saw the store through several initiatives that addressed the changing landscape of book-selling in the digital age. In 2013, Emily stepped away from the family business, but returned as the president and owner in 2019.

Readings & Events

Each month, dozens of authors, artists and thought-leaders visit Powell's for readings, panels and other events in the Pearl Room's Basil Hallward Gallery. The store also hosts children's story hours (some led by drag queens), poetry slams, book clubs, writing workshops and game demonstrations.

Rare Wonders

Powell's **Rare Book Room** (11am to 7pm) is a temple of first-edition collectables and antiquarian treasure. Resembling an old library, the 1000-sq-ft space has antique lamps that cast a warm glow, creating an elegance that's perfect for perusing the 9000-volume collection.

The oldest book is a work by Decimus Magnus Ausonius (310–395 AD) that dates back to 1494. The most expensive is a two-volume set of the first public description of the Lewis and Clark Centennial Exposition, valued at $350,000.

★ **Top Tips**

○ To wander more strategically, grab a map from the information desk, located in the Green Room.

○ For those who prefer more guidance with their browsing, Powell's offers a staff-led tour of the store at 10am on Sunday. The tour lasts 45 minutes and slots are first-come, first-served.

○ If a tour is too much, there are very helpful staff on each floor who can help you find just about any book you could think of.

✖ **Take a Break**

Powell's Coffee Room houses a branch of local cafe **World Coffee & Tea** (www.worldcup coffee.com).

There are plenty of eateries within walking distance – **Little Big Burger** (☑503-274-9008; www. littlebigburger.com; 122 NW 10th Ave; burgers $5-6; ⊙11am-10pm) for the carnivores, and Prasad (p75) for the herbivores.

Walking Tour 🚶

Nob Hill & Slabtown

In vogue with upper-crust Portlanders since the 1880s, Nob Hill is an upscale residential area filled with stately Victorian homes, trendy restaurants and homegrown boutiques. Slabtown – Portland's most recent up-and-coming district that was once industrial – houses modern high-rise condos and an ever-growing number of restaurants and bars. NW 21st and NW 23rd Aves are the arteries connecting the two districts.

Walk Facts

Start Dragontree Spa
(🚌 15)

End Breakside Brewery
(🚌 15; 🚋 NS)

Length 2 miles; five hours

❶ Spa rejuvenation

Kick things off with an indulgent spa treatment at **Dragontree** (☎503-221-4123; www.thedragontree. com; 2768 NW Thurman St; 1hr massage from $105; ⏰10am-8.15pm Sun-Fri, 9am-9pm Sat) in Slabtown. You'll emerge rejuvenated after a full-body massage – pick from Swedish or deep tissue, with the option of products infused with herbs, essential oils and even CBD; all massages include 30 minutes in the sauna. Body scrubs, facials, Ayurvedic therapies and acupuncture are also available.

❷ Baked treats

Pop into Slabtown's French bakery **St Honoré Boulangerie** (☎503-445-4342; www.sainthonorebakery. com; 2335 NW Thurman St; meals $10-14, pastries $3-6; ⏰7am-8pm) for a post-spa treat. Sample mini marionberry croissants, brioche toast with vanilla and rum custard and fresh apples, and lemon custard tarts with almond cream. Snag a table on the sidewalk and settle into the sweetness.

❸ Elite Ave

Take a stroll down **NW 23rd Ave**, the area's most buzzing street that forms the western border of Nob Hill. It's lined with loads of local businesses housed in arts-and-crafts-style storefronts, where you'll rub shoulders with Portland's elite.

❹ Neighborhood cinema

For a bit of avant-garde entertainment, head to **Cinema 21** (☎503-223-4515; www.cinema21.com; 616 NW 21st Ave) in Nob Hill. It's Portland's top pick for art-house, independent and foreign flicks – all of which you can enjoy with a beer or a glass of wine.

❺ Dinnertime eleganza

For an upscale dinner, check out **Paley's Place** (☎503-243-2403; www.paleysplace.net; 1204 NW 21st Ave; mains $23-45; ⏰5:30-10pm Mon-Thu, 5-11pm Fri & Sat, 5-10pm Sun), set in a Victorian home in Nob Hill. Run by James Beard Award–winning chef Vitaly Paley, it's been one of Portland's top picks for almost 25 years. The menu features seasonal, Pacific Northwest ingredients prepared with French and Russian influences.

❻ Beer o'clock

Stop by **Breakside Brewery** (p77) in Slabtown for a post-dinner beer. Renowned for its innovative techniques, many of its brews are laced with exotic fruits and aromatics. The tap house pours craft brews from 16 taps, including its nationally award-winning IPA. The vast space is buzzing with locals, who also enjoy the outdoor patio on a sunny day.

Northwest & the Pearl District

A **B** **C** **D**

1

NW York St

NW Roosevelt St

6

NW Wilson St

Elements
Glass

NW 27th Ave

NW 26th Ave

NW 24th Ave

NW 21st Ave

**NORTHWEST
INDUSTRIAL**

NW Wilson St

NW Vaughn St

NW Upshur St

NW 23rd Pl

12

2

NW Thurman St

NW Savier St

NW Raleigh St

15

NW Quimby St

5

NW 27th Ave

Vaux's
Swifts

NW 25th St

NW 24th Ave

NW 23rd Ave

NW 22nd Ave

NW 21st Ave

3

NW Cornell Rd

**NOB
HILL**

4

26

NW Kearney St

NW Johnson St

NW 24th Ave

NW 23rd Ave

NW Irving St

NW 21st Ave

NW Hoyt St

9

20

NW Glisan St

NW Flanders St

5

NW Everett St

W Burnside St

6

**ARLINGTON
HEIGHTS**

**GOOSE
HOLLOW**

W Burnside St

A **B** **C** **D**

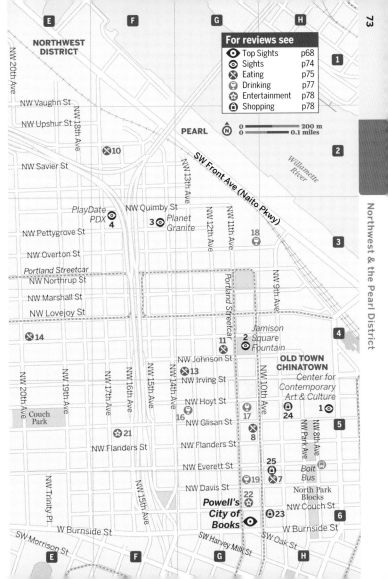

Northwest & the Pearl District

NORTHWEST DISTRICT

For reviews see
- Top Sights p68
- Sights p74
- Eating p75
- Drinking p77
- Entertainment p78
- Shopping p78

NW 20th Ave

NW Vaughn St

NW Upshur St

NW 18th Ave

PEARL

0 ——— 200 m
0 ——— 0.1 miles

NW Savier St

10

SW Front Ave (Naito Pkwy)

NW 13th Ave

Willamette River

PlayDate PDX
4

NW Quimby St

3 Planet Granite

NW 12th Ave

NW 11th Ave

18

NW Pettygrove St

NW Overton St

Portland Streetcar

NW Northrup St

NW Marshall St

NW Lovejoy St

NW 9th Ave

14

Portland Streetcar

Jamison Square Fountain
2

11

NW Johnson St

OLD TOWN CHINATOWN

13

NW Irving St

Center for Contemporary Art & Culture

NW Hoyt St

16

17

NW Glisan St

8

24

1

NW 20th Ave

NW 19th Ave

NW 17th Ave

NW 16th Ave

NW 15th Ave

NW 14th Ave

NW 10th Ave

NW Park Ave

NW 8th Ave

Couch Park

21

NW Flanders St

NW Flanders St

NW Everett St

25

Bolt Bus

19

7

NW Trinity Pl

NW Davis St

22

North Park Blocks

NW 15th Ave

Powell's City of Books

23

NW Couch St

SW Morrison St

W Burnside St

W Burnside St

SW Harvey Milk St

SW Oak St

E

F

G

H

Sights

Center for Contemporary Art & Culture
MUSEUM

1 ◎ MAP P72, H5

Home to the 1300-item collection of the former Museum of Contemporary Craft, this exhibition space at PNCA (Pacific Northwest College of Art) focuses on the role of craft and design in modern culture and presents several intriguing exhibitions each year. Check online for events and lectures open to the public. (CCAC; ☑503-226-4391; http://ccac.pnca.edu; 511 NW Broadway; admission free; ⊙11am-6pm Mon-Sat)

Jamison Square Fountain
FOUNTAIN

2 ◎ MAP P72, G4

For simple pleasures, visit the Jamison Square Fountain, a popular Pearl District oasis that attracts splashing kids. (810 NW 11th Ave; 👥; 🚋NS Line, A Loop, B Loop)

Planet Granite
CLIMBING

3 ◎ MAP P72, F3

This enormous indoor rock-climbing gym has something for every level of climber, from total newbie to expert. You'll need a belay partner to climb on the rope routes downstairs, but there's also a huge bouldering area on the 2nd floor, as well as a range of gym equipment. Also runs a full schedule of classes including yoga and Pilates. (☑503-477-5666; www.planetgranite.com; 1405 NW 14th Ave; day pass adult/child $21/15, shoes & harness rental $7; ⊙6am-11pm Mon-Fri, 8am-8pm Sat, to 6pm Sun; 🚋B Loop, NS Line)

PlayDate PDX
PLAYGROUND

4 ◎ MAP P72, F3

A huge indoor playground offering wi-fi and some refreshments. Admission is free after 5pm on Monday. (☑503-227-7529; www.playdatepdx.com; 1434 NW 17th Ave; admission $8-14, half-price under 4yr; ⊙9am-8pm Sun-Thu, to 9pm Fri & Sat; 👥)

Vaux's Swifts
BIRD-WATCHING

5 ◎ MAP P72, A3

Every September, tens of thousands of Vaux's swifts roost for the night in Chapman Elementary School's old brick chimney. Seeing them spiral down in their multitudes, right at sunset, is an unforgettable sight. (www.audubonportland.org/local-birding/swiftwatch; 1445 NW 26th Ave; ⊙dusk)

Elements Glass
ART

6 ◎ MAP P72, D1

Glass-artist wannabes can learn to make their own Christmas ornaments during the holiday season at Portland's largest glassblowing shop, just north of the Pearl District. (☑503-228-0575; www.elementsglass.com; 1979 NW Vaughn St; Christmas ornament class from $40; ⊙10am-5:30pm Mon-Fri)

Eating

Prasad

VEGAN $

7 MAP P72, H6

Prasad's location inside a yoga studio tells you a lot. Healthy, hearty salads, bowls and smoothies come in every shade of green: try the Pride of Portland (brown rice, avocado, scallions, olive oil and sauce, with a green juice) or Endless Summer (zucchini noodles, avocado-pesto cream, tomatoes, spinach, bell pepper and basil). Breakfast options include a tasty maple-chia waffle with vanilla cashew cream. (☏503-224-3993; www.prasadpdx. com; 925 NW Davis St; mains $4-12; ⏲7:30am-8pm Mon-Fri, 9am-8pm Sat & Sun; ✔; ☐77)

Northwest Art

Northwest Portland is a great place to experience the city's fine art – many top galleries are here, as well as the CCAC. It's also home to Portland's primary theater company, Portland Center Stage (p78), in addition to a couple of great cinemas. Peppered throughout are plenty of green spaces to take respite as you while your way around the super walkable area. The Pearl District hosts the **Art in the Pearl** (www.artinthepearl.com; ⊙Sep) festival each Labor Day weekend.

Jamison Square Fountain

Pho Van Fresh VIETNAMESE $

8 MAP P72, G5

This Pearl District outpost of the Pho Van chainlet serves ultra-fresh classic Vietnamese food in a no-nonsense setting. Try one of the many salad roll variations or a big warm bowl of pho. Order at the counter. (☏503-248-2172; www.phovanfresh.com; 1012 NW Glisan St; mains $8-14; ⏰11am-10pm Mon-Sat)

Muu-Muu's FUSION $$

9 MAP P72, D5

Two challenges face you at Muu-Muu's: first, deciding whether it's more of a bar or a restaurant; and second, deciding what to eat. The menu is all over the place, from seared tuna to brussels sprouts, burgers to po'boys to enchiladas to coconut curry. Avoid decisions: order several small plates and a perfect cocktail, and enjoy the scene. (☏503-223-8169; www.muumuus.net; 612 NW 21st Ave; small plates $4-9, mains $10-22; ⏰11:30am-1am Mon-Wed, to 2am Thu & Fri, 10am-2am Sat, to 1am Sun; ▣77)

Olympia Provisions FRENCH $$

10 MAP P72, F2

French-inspired rotisserie bistro serving up charcuterie and cheese boards, gourmet sandwiches, salads and deli items, and main plates such as rotisserie chicken and steamed clams. It also does delicious eggs Benedict for brunch. (☏503-894-8136; www.olympiaprov isions.com; 1632 NW Thurman St; charcuterie $17-34, sandwiches $10-18, mains $17-27; ⏰11am-10pm Mon-Fri, 9am-10pm Sat, 9am-9pm Sun; ▣16)

Piazza Italia ITALIAN $$

11 MAP P72, G4

Remember that great *ragù* you last had in Bologna or those memorable *vongole* (clams) you once polished off in Sicily? Well, here they are again at this highly authentic restaurant that succeeds where so many fail: replicating the true essence of Italian food in North America. (☏503-478-0619; www.piazzaportland.com; 1129 NW Johnson St; pasta $12-16; ⏰11:30am-3pm daily, plus 5-9:30pm Sun-Tue, 5-10pm Wed & Thu, 5-11pm Fri & Sat)

Ataula SPANISH $$$

12 MAP P72, C2

This critically acclaimed Spanish tapas restaurant offers outstanding cuisine. If they are on the menu, try the *nuestras bravas* (sliced, fried potatoes in milk aioli), *croquetas* (salt-cod fritters) and *xupa xup* (chorizo 'lollipop'). Great cocktails, too. Be sure to reserve. (☏503-894-8904; www.ataulapdx.com; 1818 NW 23rd Pl; tapas $9-17, paella dishes $35-40; ⏰4:30-10pm Tue-Sat; ▣15, 77)

Irving Street Kitchen MODERN AMERICAN $$$

13 MAP P72, G4

This upscale restaurant serves Pacific Northwest cuisine with a Southern touch, with exceptional dishes like braised beef cheeks with horseradish and parsnip puree, and arugula and sheep's-cheese crepes with pickled corn. Save room for the butterscotch pudding served in Mason jars. The wine list is also notable. It does brunch too. (☎503-343-9440; www.irvingstreetkitchen.com; 701 NW 13th Ave; mains $21-30; ☺5:30-10pm Mon-Fri, 10am-2:30pm & 5:30-11pm Sat & Sun)

Café Nell
AMERICAN $$$

14 ❌ MAP P72, E4

This little bistro in Nob Hill is both cozy and sophisticated. Large portions of comfort food range from breakfast omelets and oysters on the half shell to wild mushroom risotto and grilled salmon. Happy hour means classic cocktails, frites and tacos. (☎503-295-6487; www.cafenell.com; 1987 NW Kearney; mains $19-26; ☺11am-10pm Mon-Fri, 9am-10pm Sat, 9am-8pm Sun)

Drinking

Breakside Brewery
BREWERY

15 🍺 MAP P72, D3

Known for experimental brews laced with fruits, vegetables and spices, plus a nationally lauded IPA, Breakside expanded beyond its original location in northeast Portland and opened a bigger venue in Slabtown in 2017. Sixteen taps, great grub and two levels of seating (plus a large patio) in a cheery industrial space make it one of Portland's finest brewpubs. (☎503-444-7597; www.breakside.com; 1570 NW 22nd Ave; ☺11am-10pm Sun-Thu, to 11pm Fri & Sat; 🚌8)

Barista
COFFEE

16 🍺 MAP P72, G5

A truly excellent coffee shop, this tiny, stylish shop is owned by award-winning barista Billy Wilson. Beans are sourced from specialty roasters. Three other locations in town. (☎503-274-1211; www.baristapdx.com; 539 NW 13th Ave; ☺6am-7pm Mon-Fri, from 7am Sat & Sun; 🚌77)

Lowbrow Lounge
BAR

17 🍺 MAP P72, G5

A dark, divey oasis holding its ground against the encroaching condo-ization of the neighborhood, the Lowbrow is old-school Portland at its best: weird art, great beer, friendly and unfussy bartenders, better-than-dive-standard food at good prices. If you're meeting someone there, it's fun to arrive first, sit toward the back, and watch your friend stumble in blinded until their eyes adjust to the darkness. (☎503-226-0200; www.lowbrowlounge.com; 1036 NW Hoyt St; ☺3pm-2:30am Mon-Sat; 🚌77)

Ovation
COFFEE

18 🍺 MAP P72, G3

Stop in for a warming Moroccan spice latte at this airy, glassed-in coffee shop, with tempting pastries and friendly staff. Other Moroccan-leaning treats include mint tea and a pistachio latte. The shop is right beside the Fields park, anchoring

Easy as A, B, C

Collectively, Nob Hill and Slabtown are referred to as the **Alphabet District**. The street names are in alphabetical order, starting southerly with Burnside St, which spans the entire area, up to northernmost York St in Slabtown. Fans of the *Simpsons* will note some familiar names here (creator Matt Groening is from Portland), such as Flanders, Lovejoy and Quimby Sts.

the northeastern corner of the Pearl District. (☏503-719-7716; www.ovationpdx.com; 941 NW Overton St; ◷6am-6pm Mon-Fri, 7am-5pm Sat & Sun; 🚊NS Loop, B Loop)

Deschutes Brewery   BREWERY

19 MAP P72, G6

This is a branch of the Bend brewery, but the stuff is brewed here, too – which keeps pints fresh and tasty in all 26 taps. The Mirror Pond Ale and Obsidian Stout have won 'best of show' at the International Brewing Awards, and the Fresh Squeezed IPA is brilliant. (☏503-296-4906; www.deschutesbrewery.com; 210 NW 11th Ave; ◷11am-10pm, to midnight Fri & Sat)

Sterling Coffee Roasters   COFFEE

20 MAP P72, D5

Elegant coffee shop roasting complex with flavorful beans. The menu is simple, with great cappuccinos and espressos by knowledgeable baristas. (☏503-248-2133; www.sterlingcoffeeroasters.com; 518 NW 21st Ave; ◷6am-5pm Mon-Fri, from 8am Sat & Sun)

Entertainment

Mission Theater   CINEMA

21 MAP P72, F5

Come early for a front-row balcony seat at this beautiful McMenamins theater, with mostly second-run movies and lectures. (☏503-223-4527; www.mcmenamins.com; 1624 NW Glisan St)

Portland Center Stage   THEATER

22 MAP P72, G6

The city's main theater company performs in the Portland Armory – a renovated Pearl District landmark with state-of-the-art features. (☏503-445-3700; www.pcs.org; 128 NW 11th Ave; tickets from $25; 🚊4, 8, 44, 77)

Shopping

MadeHere PDX   CONCEPT STORE

23 MAP P72, H6

This expansive shop in the Pearl sources from more than 280 different suppliers, all based in the Pacific Northwest. Everything is made locally, from fancy soaps and luxury chocolates to snowboards, backpacks, leather goods and rugged outdoor clothing. Sales staff know the backstory of each supplier, and there's a definite sense of

Shopping

The Armory, home of Portland Center Stage

community. (503-224-0122; www.
madehereonline.com; 40 NW 10th Ave;
11am-6pm Sun-Wed & Fri, to 7pm
Thu, 10am-7pm Sat; 20, B Loop,
NS Line)

Thelonius Wines ALCOHOL

24 MAP P72, H5

A very cute wine shop in the Pearl
that doubles as a tasting room,
Thelonius was started by an Argen-
tine with a long resume in Pacific
Northwest wineries. Like practically everywhere these days, the
shop's primary focus is on natural
and organic wines. Tastings are
scheduled every Friday from 6pm
to 8pm and occasionally on Monday and Tuesday. (503-444-7747;
www.theloniouswines.com; 516 NW 9th
Ave; 4-9pm Mon-Fri, noon-9pm Sat,
noon-7pm Sun; 77)

Halo Shoes SHOES

25 MAP P72, H5

Gorgeous, high-end designer shoes
for both women and men, with
knowledgeable service personnel to
go along. You'll need a very fat wal-
let, but you won't get better-quality
shoes. Sells nice handbags, too.
(503-331-0366; www.haloshoes.
com; 938 NW Everett St; 11am-6pm
Mon-Sat, noon-5pm Sun)

MudPuddles Toys & Books TOYS

26 MAP P72, C4

Educational toys and books
as well as all the latest for the
kids. (503-224-5586; www.
mudpuddlestoys.com; 2305 NW Kearney St; 10am-6pm Mon-Thu, to 7pm
Fri & Sat, 11am-5pm Sun)

Top Sight 📷
Forest Park

Covering more than 5100 acres on the eastern slope of the Tualatin Mountains is Forest Park, the largest wooded urban park in the US. Flanking Portland's West Hills, its 70-mile network of verdant trails are a great way to witness the grandeur of the Pacific Northwest's forestlands without having to leave the city limits.

☎ 503-223-5449

www.forestpark
conservancy.org

🚌 15, 20

Hit the Trails

Connecting top sights like Washington Park, the Audubon Society and Pittock Mansion, Forest Park's Wildwood Trail is an impressive 30-miles long. Rolling through the woods, the trail is intersected by shorter trails, streams, roads and fire lanes.

The Lower MacLeay Trail is good for Forest Park first-timers. Set in a canyon along Balch Creek, it offers an explosion of lush plant life and majestic trees – including the country's tallest fir tree located within an urban area, a 242ft high giant that can be found near the lichen-coated, 1930s Stone House (pictured). The trail is an easy 1.8-mile round trip, and can be accessed via Lower Macleay Park, located at the westernmost end of NW Upshur St in Northwest Portland.

Pittock Mansion

This grand 1914 **mansion** (☏503-823-3623; www.pittockmansion.org; 3229 NW Pittock Dr; adult/child $12/8; ◷10am-4pm late Sep-Dec & Feb-May, 10am-5pm June-late Sep; Ⓟ) was built by pioneer-entrepreneur Henry Pittock, who revitalized the *Oregonian* newspaper; his wife Georgiana started Portland's annual Rose Festivals. Guided tours are available, but it's also worth visiting the grounds (free) to have a picnic while taking in the spectacular views. The mansion lies along the Wildwood Trail with dozens of miles of connecting trails branching off it.

Wildlife Spotting

Forest Park is a refuge for 62 mammal species, including black-tailed deer, creeping voles, northern flying squirrels, pocket gophers, Roosevelt elk, Pacific jumping mice and more.

More than 112 bird species take refuge in Forest Park's tree canopy, including northern pygmy and great horned owls and hairy woodpeckers.

★ **Top Tips**

o Biking and horseback riding is permitted only on certain trails – check the Forest Park Conservancy (www.forestpark conservancy.org) website.

o The Portland Parks & Recreation (www.portlandoregon.gov/parks) website has a high-resolution trail map available for download.

✕ **Take a Break**

There's nothing in the way of refreshments in the park, but if you find yourself in the vicinity of the **Audubon Society** (☏503-292-6855; www.audubonportland.org; ◷10am-6pm Mon-Sat, to 5pm Sun), the Nature Store sometimes stocks locally made snacks.

★ **Getting There**

Many of the trailheads are only accessible by car. Check the Portland Parks & Recreation website for specific locations.

Explore ◈

Northeast

Northeast Portland is home to some of the city's most vibrant, ethnically diverse communities. A stretch of Alberta St makes up the Alberta Arts District that all host a wealth of restaurants, bars, galleries and boutiques. Neighborhoods like Irvington feature stately historic residences, while north of the city the thoroughfares of Mississippi Ave and N Williams Ave form the Mississippi-Williams District.

The Short List

○ **Alberta Arts District (p84)** *Wandering blocks of galleries and studios alongside creative locals.*

○ **Mississippi-Williams District (p95)** *Checking out up-and-coming bands at places like Mississippi Studios and dining at restaurants in one of Portland's most rapidly developing areas.*

○ **Hollywood Theatre (p95)** *Taking in a film at this art deco movie house, all while eating pizza and sipping a microbrew.*

○ **Coffee shops (p93)** *Cozying up with a strong espresso and a good book at a local java house.*

○ **Breweries (p94)** *Sampling flights of inventive suds at chill neighborhood breweries.*

Getting There & Around

🚆 The MAX light-rail Red, Blue, Green and Yellow lines stop at Rose Quarter Transit Center, located across from the Moda Center. The Red, Blue and Green lines stop at Lloyd Center.

🚌 From the city center, route 8 runs north along NE 15th, with stops at the Lloyd Center and continuing up past Alberta St.

Neighborhood Map on p88

Mississippi Avenue GREG VAUGHN/ALAMY STOCK PHOTO ©

Top Sight 📷

Alberta Arts District

In Northeast Portland, the stretch of Alberta St from MLK Jr Blvd to 30th Ave is a corridor of diverse local culture known as the Alberta Arts District. Lined with art galleries, boutiques, restaurants and bars, the main drag is known for its monthly 'Last Thursday' street fair event, but the area is worth exploring any day of the month.

👁 **MAP P88, D2**

🚌 Route 72 runs along Alberta St from MLK Blvd to NE 30th Ave. From downtown, route 8 travels up 15th Ave and stops at the intersection of Alberta St.

History

Community development task forces were created in 1993 to reinvigorate the Alberta area, which had suffered from disinvestment and segregation for several decades. Focus was placed on providing low-income housing, as well as establishing and empowering neighborhood-oriented and minority-owned small businesses. Artists were drawn to the neighborhood thanks to cheap rents. Residences and studios were set up, and the influx helped spur commercial growth in storefronts that were previously boarded up. By 1997, the neighborhood was home to a thriving creative community.

Last Thursday

Since 1997, the **Last Thursday on Alberta** (📋503-823-1052; www.lastthurspdx.org; ⏰6-9pm) art walk has drawn crowds to Alberta St for a dose of creative culture. With buskers, bands, acrobatic troupes and visitors of all stripes, the affair makes for fantastic people-watching.

Held throughout the year the event ramps up in the summertime. The 15-block stretch of Alberta St (from 15th to 30th Avenues) closes to vehicular traffic from 6pm to 9pm on the last Thursdays of June, July and August. Crowds fill the street as people wander gallery openings and local businesses' art exhibitions. Independent vendors sell their wares along the sidewalks, and there's plenty of food and drink too.

Street Art

Public art adds to the vibrant character of Alberta St, where you'll see bold graffiti, colorful murals, and functional spaces like parking spots reimagined with a creative twist.

The Alberta area was once home to one of the highest populations of African Americans in Portland, who survived a history of segregation and redlining – in addition to today's struggles of gentrification. Much of the public art in this area illustrates realities of this community.

★ Top Tips

Alberta St is a prime location for taking in some of Portland's best street art. The Portland Street Art Alliance (www.pdxstreetart.org/finding-street-art) has a free map available for download that features an index of all the street's murals.

✕ Take a Break

Alberta St is peppered with plenty of places to eat. Proud Mary (p93) is a top pick for excellent coffee, fresh juices and smoothies, and Insta-worthy brunch plates.

For great Indian, check out Bollywood Theater (p92). Podnah's Pit (p92), a few blocks away on NE Killingsworth, has some of the best BBQ in the city.

Walking Tour 🥾

Northeast Wellness Walkabout

*Northeast Portland is home to locally owned
restaurants, shops and galleries, and though
it's extremely gentrified, it's also where you'll
encounter the most Portlanders from different
backgrounds. There are great ethnic eateries
along Alberta St, frequented mostly by hip, young
creatives, as well as bars with more mellow,
hometown vibes.*

Walk Facts

Start Green Hop
(🚌 8, 17)

End Beast (🚌 72)

Length 2 miles; six hours

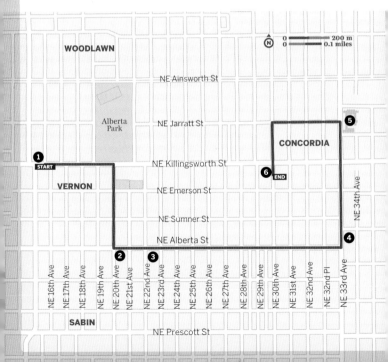

❶ Hip-Hop & weed

Begin this day of wellness at **Green Hop** (📞971-301-5859; www.gogreenhop.com; 5515 NE 16th Ave; ⏰8:30am-9:45pm), a dispensary where hip-hop, art and cannabis collide. It's a venture of many firsts: Oregon's first black-owned dispensary, the first co-owned by a black female, and the world's first hip-hop-themed dispensary. Elevate your consciousness with a strain named after a musician, or opt for non-psychoactive CBD gummies to retain a clear head.

❷ Aussie-style avo toast

Make your way to **Proud Mary** (p93), the first US location of the renowned Australian coffee roaster's cafe. For light but filling nosh, order the artfully plated avocado toast. Wash it down with a flat white or other espresso-based drink to get you out the door.

❸ French-pressed fuel

Next, head two blocks east to **Sip**, (📞503-680-5639; www.sipjuicecart.com; 2210 NE Alberta St; drinks $3-8; ⏰8am-5pm Mon-Thu, to 6pm Sun), a juice bar housed in a renovated camper van that's permanently parked along Alberta St between 22nd and 23rd Aves. Grab a fresh green or fruit juice to go and down it on your way to the next stop – you'll need to stay plenty hydrated.

❹ Soak & sauna

Spend the next couple of hours at **Common Ground** (📞503-238-1065; www.cgwc.org; 5010 NE 33rd; 1hr soak $17; ⏰10am-11pm, last entry 10pm), a co-op with a soaking tub, sauna and a team of wellness providers that specialize in massage, acupuncture, naturopathic medicine and more. All experiences here are clothing-optional, so feel free to let it all hang out if it suits – or bring a suit if it doesn't.

❺ School flicks & chill

Once you're sufficiently relaxed, head to the **Kennedy School Theater** (📞503-249-3983; www.mcmenamins.com; 5736 NE 33rd Ave; adult/child $5/3) for a matinee flick on a comfy sofa. Screening mostly second-run features, this historic theater was once a school auditorium. Unwind even more with a craft beer or a glass of wine. There's pizza and other pub fare if you find yourself peckish, but don't fill up – better eats await.

❻ Save the Beast for last

Finish the day by treating yourself to a six-course feast at **Beast** (p93), featuring a local produce-driven menu that changes every couple of weeks to reflect the Pacific Northwest's best seasonal ingredients.

Northeast

A
B
C
D

N Albina Ave

19

500 m
0.25 miles

N Killingsworth St
NE Killingsworth St

NE 15th Ave

Alberta
Park

10

VERNON

N Alberta St

Everybody's
Bike Rentals
& Tours

2

NE Webster St
NE Alberta St

33

NE Wygant St

King
School
Park

KING

Alberta
Arts
District

31

16

NE Going St

NE Going St

NE Prescott St

N Skidmore St

NE Skidmore St

NE Mason St

NE Mason St

SABIN

N Shaver St

27
32
34

Denorval
Unthank
City Park

15

NE Failing St

NE 13th Ave
NE 15th Ave
NE 17th Ave
NE 19th Ave

36

BOISE

21

N Fremont St

18

9

NE Fremont St

IRVINGTON

N Cook St

Irving
Park

N Mississippi Ave

NE Siskiyou St

N Missouri Ave

N Borthwick Ave

N Williams Ave

N Rodney Ave

Matt Dishman
Community
Center & Indoor Pool

3

4

Portland's
Culinary
Workshop

NE Knott St
NE Russell St

ELIOT

25

NE Knott St

NE 15th Ave
NE 17th Ave
NE 19th Ave

12

Albina/Mississippi

13

NE Thompson St

NE Tillamook St

N Mississippi Ave

NE Hancock St

NE Hancock St

Interstate Ave

NE Broadway St

5

Willamette
River

22

NE Broadway St

35

LLOYD

NE Halsey St

N Broadway

Rose
Quarter
Transit
Center

26

Interstate
Rose
Quarter

Holladay
Park

NE 7th

Union
Station
(Amtrak)

6

NW
Hoyt

Greyhound

Oregon
Convention
Center

Convention
Center

1

Lloyd Center/
NE 11th

KERNS

NE Irving St

A
B
C
D

Northeast

NE Jarratt St

NE Killingsworth St · 14

NE Killingsworth St

29

NE Emerson St

NE Emerson St

11

NE Sumner St

NE Webster St

8

NE Alberta St

NE Alberta Ct

NE Wygant St

NE Going St

6 CULLY

NE Going St

NE Prescott St

NE Prescott St

NE Mason St

Wilshire Park

NE 30th Ave

NE 33rd Ave

NE 42nd Ave

NE 47th Ave

ALAMEDA

NE Shaver St

BEAUMONT-WILSHIRE

Rose City Cemetery

NE Fremont St

NE Fremont St

NE Klickitat St

NE 41st Ave

NE Siskiyou St

NE Siskiyou St

NE 33rd Ave

NE Stanton St

NE Stanton St

NE Knott St

NE 42nd Ave

US Grant 5 Grant Park · Outdoor Pool

NE Brazee St 23

NE Thompson St

NE Thompson St

GRANT PARK

NE US Grant Pl

NE Sandy Blvd

ROSE CITY PARK

NE Hancock St

17

NE 24th Ave

20

NE Schuyler St

28

NE Broadway St

24

NE Broadway St

SULLIVAN'S GULCH

7 HOLLYWOOD

NE Halsey St

LAURELHURST

Hollywood Transit Center

NE 33rd Ave

NE César E Chávez Blvd

NE 47th Ave

Frazer Park

Banfield Expy

NE Sandy Blvd

Oregon Park

For reviews see

◉	Top Sights	p84
◉	Sights	p90
✕	Eating	p90
☕	Drinking	p93
★	Entertainment	p95
🔒	Shopping	p96

Sights

Oregon Convention Center
NOTABLE BUILDING

1 ◉ MAP P88, B6

Those two glass spires you can see from downtown identify this huge multipurpose building where some of Portland's largest events are held. Check the website for a calendar. (www.oregoncc.org; 777 NE Martin Luther King Jr Blvd; ☒Red, Blue, Green, Yellow)

Everybody's Bike Rentals & Tours
CYCLING

2 ◉ MAP P88, B2

It's true that Portland is best seen by bicycle, and this company offers low-key, fun tours of the city and its surroundings – whether you're into food and farms or beer and parks. Try the 'Beyond Portlandia' tour for an off-the-beaten-path glimpse of the city. Bicycle rentals, from commuters to mountain bikes, are also available. (☎503-358-0152; www.pdxbikerentals.com; 305 NE Wygant St; rentals per hour $8-25, tours per person from $39; ⏱10am-5pm; ☒6)

Matt Dishman Community Center & Indoor Pool
SWIMMING

3 ◉ MAP P88, B4

Swimmers should grab their suits and make a beeline to the indoor pool here; it's just north of the Lloyd District. Check hours beforehand. (☎503-823-3673; www.portland

oregon.gov/parks/60933; 77 NE Knott St; drop-in visit adult/child $6/4)

Portland's Culinary Workshop
COOKING

4 ◉ MAP P88, A4

From beginner to professional cooking courses, including seafood, barbecuing, Mexican, Thai, gluten-free, pastries and cakes. (☎503-512-0447; www.portlandsculinary workshop.com; 807 N Russell St; per person from $65)

Grant Outdoor Pool
SWIMMING

5 ◉ MAP P88, F4

There's an outdoor swimming pool at US Grant Park. The pool is only open in summer; check online for exact dates. (☎503-823-3674; www.portlandoregon.gov/parks/61021; 2300 NE 33rd Ave; adult/child $4.75/3.75; ⏱Jun-Sep; ☒70)

Eating

Yonder
SOUTHERN US $

6 ◉ MAP P88, G2

Yonder's excellent fried chicken is available 'dusted' (adorned with dry spice), 'dipped' (tossed in a zesty sauce) or 'hot' (just spicy enough to be memorable, without injury), served with cornbread or a biscuit with sweet sorghum butter. Add a side of pimento mac and cheese or bacon braised collard greens, then wash it down with a craft cocktail. Down-home good! (☎503-444-7947; www.yonderpdx.com; 4636 NE

42nd Ave; mains $8-17; ⏱11am-9pm Wed-Sun)

Chin's Kitchen

CHINESE $

7 🗺 MAP P88, G5

Not so long ago, Chin's was known mostly for its iconic neon sign. But under new owners – two sisters from the city of Harbin in northern China – the humble restaurant has been churning out dumplings to die for. There are also hand-pulled noodles, stews and other well-executed regional dishes making local critics swoon. (📞503-281-1203; www.portlandchinskitchen.com; 4132 NE Broadway; mains $10-16; ⏱11:30am-2:30pm & 5-9pm; 🚊Red, Blue)

Pine State Biscuits

SOUTHERN US $

8 🗺 MAP P88, E2

Immensely popular for its hangover-sopping fried chicken, bacon and cheese biscuit sandwiches, with egg and gravy additions for the strong of heart. Plenty of sides, with interesting drinks like local apple cider or gourmet chocolate milk. (📞503-477-6605; www.pinestatebiscuits.com; 2204 NE Alberta St; biscuit sandwiches $6-11; ⏱7am-3pm)

Akadi PDX

AFRICAN $$

9 🗺 MAP P88, B3

Akadi chef-owner Fatou Ouattara brings the flavors of her native Ivory Coast and other West African

Northeast Eating

Oregon Convention Center

ARCHITECTS: ZGF; IMAGE: VICTORIA DITKOVSKY/SHUTTERSTOCK ©

Diverse Eats

As the city's most culturally diverse area, Northeast Portland features some of the best ethnic food in town. From food carts to atmospheric neighborhood eateries, you'll find everything from hand-pulled Chinese noodles to West African staples like jolof rice. Many top-rated fine-dining establishments are also located here, offering world-class culinary experiences with a side of hometown charm.

countries to Portland, where you'll find devoted locals enjoying authentic dishes at kente-cloth-covered tables in the low-key dining room. Samusas, cassava sticks, and jolof rice plates are crowd-pleasing entry points, but the flavor-rich traditional stews (eaten with fufu) are truly where it's at. (📞503-477-7138; www.akadipdx.com; 3601 NE Martin Luther King Jr Blvd; mains $13-19; ⏰noon-10pm Tue-Sun)

Podnah's Pit BARBECUE $$

10 MAP P88, D1

Possibly Portland's best barbecue joint, serving amazingly tender and tasty pork ribs that have been smoked for four hours. There's also brisket, chicken and pulled-pork sandwiches, along with typical sides such as coleslaw, potato salad and collard greens. (📞503-281-3700; www.podnahspit.com; 1625

NE Killingsworth St; mains $14-32; ⏰11am-9pm Mon-Thu, to 10pm Fri, 9am-10pm Sat, 9am-9pm Sun; 🚌8)

Bollywood Theater INDIAN $$

11 MAP P88, E1

This popular Indian restaurant serves up 'street food' such as lamb samosas and kati rolls (meat and chutney rolled up in flatbread), along with small plates (chicken curry, pork vindaloo) and thalis (traditional set meals of various dishes). Plenty of vegetable and side dishes as well; wash it all down with a chai, a yogurt lassi or an Indian cocktail. (📞971-200-4711; www.bollywoodtheaterpdx.com; 2039 NE Alberta St; small plates $11-15, thalis $17-20; ⏰11am-10pm; 🚶; 🚌72)

Toro Bravo SPANISH $$

12 🍴 MAP P88, B4

Sure, you could order the house bacon and manchego (sheep's cheese) burger here and be happy, but it's the endless list of tapas that should guide your taste buds – get the patatas bravas, jamon croquettes or octopus a la plancha. Be prepared for a wait – this place has an enduring reputation for deliciousness. (📞503-281-4464; www.torobravopdx.com; 120 NE Russell St; tapas $3-17, mains $13-24; ⏰5-10pm Mon-Thu, to 11pm Fri & Sat)

Ox STEAK $$$

13 🍴 MAP P88, B5

One of Portland's most popular restaurants is this upscale, Argentine-inspired steakhouse.

Start with the smoked bone-marrow clam chowder, then go for the gusto: the grass-fed beef rib eye. If there's two of you, the *asado* (barbecue grill; $94) is a good choice, allowing you to try several different cuts. Reserve ahead. (☎503-284-3366; www.oxpdx.com; 2225 NE Martin Luther King Jr Blvd; mains $14-56; ☺5-10pm Sun-Thu, to 11pm Fri & Sat; 🚌6)

Beast

AMERICAN $$$

14 MAP P88, F1

At Beast, celebrated local chef Naomi Pomeroy – who went from staging underground supper-club dinners to appearing on *Top Chef* and winning a James Beard Award – offers a set fixed-price menu of six courses, wine pairings optional. Dining here is an event. Expect wildly creative use of carefully sourced ingredients, and a lot of meat. Reserve ahead. (☎503-841-6968; www.beastpdx.com; 5425 NE 30th Ave; dinner without/with wine $118/168, brunch $40/60; ☺dinner 6pm & 7:30pm Wed & Thu, 6pm & 8:45pm Fri & Sat, 7pm Sun, brunch 10am, 11:30am & 1pm Sun; 🚌72)

Ned Ludd

AMERICAN $$$

15 MAP P88, B3

Quintessentially Portland, this offbeat, upscale joint exudes thick artisan vibes, from its rustic-peasant decor to the prominent brick wood-fired oven where all dishes are cooked. The beautifully presented small plates are rotated daily. This is not a place to simply fill your tummy but one in which to sample eclectic 'American craft' delicacies. (☎503-288-6900; www.nedluddpdx.com; 3925 NE Martin Luther King Jr Blvd; small plates $3-18, mains $25-28; ☺5-9pm Sun-Thu, to 10pm Fri & Sat; 🚌6)

Drinking

Proud Mary

CAFE

16 MAP P88, D2

From the land of flat whites and avocado toast comes Proud Mary, the notable Melbourne-based coffee roaster that aptly chose Portland for its first US outpost. In addition to superb coffee, it slings delicious breakfast, brunch and lunch plates like vanilla and ricotta hotcakes, a smoked pork-belly satay sandwich and Aussie meat pies. Smoothies and fresh juices, too. (☎503-208-3475; www.proudmarycoffee.com; 2012 NE Alberta St; ☺7am-4pm Mon-Fri, from 8am Sat & Sun)

Moon & Sixpence

PUB

17 MAP P88, G5

Topping the short list of places in Portland where you can get a proper pint of Guinness is this lovely old-fashioned pub, with good fish-and-chips, friendly but not overly attentive service, darts in the back, old books to borrow, and a huge patio outside for when the rain lets up. On a gray Portland day it's hard to do better. (2014 NE 42nd Ave; ☺3pm-2:30am)

Ecliptic Brewing BREWERY

18 MAP P88, A3

It's in kind of a chilly industrial space, but the beer speaks for itself – Ecliptic was founded by John Harris, who previously brewed for McMenamins, Deschutes and Full Sail. The brewery's astronomically named creations (such as the Craft Beer medal-winning Spica Pilsner) are ambitious and wildly successful. Food includes lamb picatta, tempura asparagus and a goat's cheese and beet melt sandwich. (503-265-8002; www.eclipticbrewing.com; 825 N Cook St; 11am-10pm Sun-Thu, to 11pm Fri & Sat; 4)

Saraveza BREWERY

19 MAP P88, A1

Saraveza is a bottle shop and pub best known for its American craft beer, served by award-winning 'beertenders.' Choose from over 250 bottles of the stuff, including nine on draft. Also good for its savory and sweet pasties (hand pies). (503-206-4252; www.saraveza.com; 1004 N Killingsworth St; 11am-midnight)

Hale Pele BAR

20 MAP P88, E5

The kitschy tiki bar (aren't they all?) to come to for 'historical' tropical cocktails, all made from fresh juices, handcrafted syrups and premium spirits. Try the popular Suffering Bastard, made with ginger beer, bourbon, gin and lime.

(503-662-8454; www.halepele.com; 2733 NE Broadway; 4pm-close)

Ristretto Roasters COFFEE

21 MAP P88, B3

Medium-roast, small-batch and single-origin coffee beans that result in a mellow, more subtle cup of java. The cafe features modern wood paneling, clean lines and a huge garage door. Also at 555 NE Couch St and 222 SW Columbia Street (in Koin Tower). (503-288-8667; www.rrpdx.com; 3808 N Williams Ave; 6:30am-6pm Mon-Sat, 7am-6pm Sun;)

Upright Brewing BREWERY

22 MAP P88, B5

This basement brewery has an intimate tasting room for sampling French and Belgian farmhouse-inspired ales. (www.uprightbrewing.com; 240 N Broadway, Suite 2; 4:30-9pm Thu & Fri, 1-8pm Sat & Sun)

Laurelwood Brewing Co BREWERY

23 MAP P88, H4

The rare brewpub that's actively kid-friendly, Laurelwood makes an excellent line of beers, especially the Free Range Red and the IRA. There's a small deck upstairs in good weather, and decent pub grub. Also at 6716 SE Milwaukie Ave and inside Portland airport. (503-282-0622; www.laurelwoodbrewpub.com; 5115 NE Sandy Blvd; 11am-10pm; ; 12)

Entertainment

Hollywood Theatre CINEMA

 24 MAP P88, G5

This historic art deco cinema has excellent programming, with classic, foreign and quirky independent movies and a reverence for film over digital – it's the only place in town capable of showing movies in 70mm. Several great monthly series, including Queer Horror, B-Movie Bingo and the awesome Kung Fu Cinema, screen rare 35mm classics. There's also pizza and other grub available, plus craft beer on tap to wash it all down. (503-493-1128; www.hollywoodtheatre.org; 4122 NE Sandy Blvd)

Hollywood Theatre

Wonder Ballroom LIVE MUSIC

25 MAP P88, B4

Great live-music venue with good sound quality, excellent lineup of bands and a tiny cafe downstairs. (www.wonderballroom.com; 128 NE Russell St)

Moda Center STADIUM

26 MAP P88, B6

Formerly named the Rose Garden, this large arena is home to Portland's professional basketball team, the Trail Blazers. (503-235-8771; www.rosequarter.com/venue/moda-center; 1 N Center Court St; Yellow)

Portland Winterhawks SPECTATOR SPORT

Beervana's major-junior hockey team usually plays at the Moda Center. (503-238-6366; www.winterhawks.com; from $35)

Trail Blazers SPECTATOR SPORT

Rip City's major league basketball team plays at the Moda Center. (www.nba.com/blazers; from $38)

Mississippi Studios LIVE MUSIC

27 MAP P88, A3

This intimate bar is good for checking out budding acoustic talent along with more established musical acts. Excellent sound system. Located right on busy N Mississippi Ave.

The venue's adjacent Bar Bar pours drinks and serves awesome burgers from 11am to 2am, seven days a week. (503-288-3895; www.mississippistudios.com; 3939 N Mississippi Ave; 4)

Shopping Strips

You'll find several indie retailers and boutiques along Alberta St, Mississippi Ave and N Williams Ave. Further south, Broadway St features a decent selection of local shops, and the Lloyd District is home to the Lloyd Center mall.

Shopping

Ray's Ragtime   VINTAGE

28 🔒 MAP P88, G5

After 30 years in its downtown location this beloved vintage clothing store was on the brink of closing due to rent increases – but it relocated instead. Its inventory is heavy on the '40s through '70s, and the owner has a background in theater – many of his customers are film and TV stylists – so you know the quality is tops. (📞503-226-2616; www.raysragtimehollywood.com; 4059 NE Sandy Blvd; ⊙noon-8pm Mon-Sat, 1-6pm Sun; 🚌12)

Uplift Botanicals   DISPENSARY

29 🔒 MAP P88, F1

You can buy edibles, tinctures and pre-rolled marijuana cigarettes, plus the 'tools of the trade,' at this friendly and unintimidating shop just off Killingsworth. (📞971-319-6118; www.upliftbotanicals.com; 5421 NE 33rd Ave; ⊙9am-10pm)

Paxton Gate   ARTS & CRAFTS

30 🔒 MAP P88, A2

A warning to the squeamish: a snarling fox, a smiling warthog and a gape-mouthed hippo are just a few of the stuffed animals lining the walls here, but this curio shop is not to be missed. Celebrating a fascination with the natural world rather than the desire to capture it, this shop has everything from fossilized mollusks to vintage boiling flasks.

Taxidermy specimens are also for sale, but the shop assures its customers that these items are sourced from animals that have died from natural causes or were humanely euthanized to manage wild populations. (📞503-719-4508; www.paxtongate.com; 4204 N Mississippi Ave; ⊙11am-7pm; 🚌4)

Community Cycling Center   SPORTS & OUTDOORS

31 🔒 MAP P88, D2

You can feel good about shopping at this community bicycle shop, which has a series of programs and classes to help cyclists – especially kids – become competent riders and mechanics. Used bikes, parts and accessories are for sale, and there's a repair shop. (📞503-287-8786; www.communitycyclingcenter.org; 1700 NE Alberta St; ⊙10am-7pm)

Land   GIFTS & SOUVENIRS

32 🔒 MAP P88, A3

Land sells unique, fun and crafty gifts like tote bags, coffee mugs, greeting cards and prints, plus there's an art gallery upstairs. Famous as the setting for the *Portlandia* 'Put a Bird on It' skit. (☏503-451-0689; www.landpdx.com; 3925 N Mississippi Ave; ⊙10am-6pm)

Frock Boutique CLOTHING

33 🅐 MAP P88, D1

One of Alberta St's most whimsical and eclectic clothing stores, Frock Boutique stocks screen-printed T-shirts, sundresses, woolen hats, patterned socks, jewelry, onesies for babies and more (even for the guys). (☏503-595-0379; www.frockboutique. com; 1439 NE Alberta St; ⊙10am-6pm Tue-Sat, to 5pm Sun & Mon)

Flutter GIFTS & SOUVENIRS

34 🅐 MAP P88, A3

This cool N Mississippi Ave shop sells reclaimed and refurbished items for the home, vintage jewelry, birdcages, gothic wedding gowns, ornate pillows and feathery hats. (☏503-288-1649; www.flutter clutter.com; 3948 N Mississippi Ave; ⊙11am-7pm Mon-Wed, to 8pm Thu & Fri, 10am-8pm Sat, 10am-7pm Sun)

Broadway Books BOOKS

35 🅐 MAP P88, D5

A good general, independent bookstore with especially strong literary fiction, biography and nonfiction sections. Holds frequent author readings. (☏503-284-1726; www. broadwaybooks.net; 1714 NE Broadway; ⊙10am-7pm Mon-Sat, to 5pm Sun)

Pistils Nursery ARTS & CRAFTS

36 🅐 MAP P88, A3

Looking for your next terrarium? Something to spruce up your rooftop beehive? This N Mississippi Ave shop has everything for the urban homesteader. Peruse what's needed to create your own farm oasis, including exotic plants, terrariums and accessories. If all the flora sparks ambitions for exercising your green thumb, ask about workshops and in-store events. (☏503-288-4889; http:// pistilsnursery.com; 3811 N Mississippi Ave; ⊙10am-7pm)

Walking Tour 🥾

Kerns: The In-Between Zone

Nestled between the city's Northeast and Southeast quadrants, this in-between district blends industrial grit with quaint, hyperlocal charm. New apartment builds, arts-and-crafts multiplexes and single-family bungalows house a mix of residents, and shops and restaurants dot the main drags, from the northern side of E Burnside St up to NE Glisan St and Sandy Blvd, all connected by bustling NE 28th.

Walk Facts

Start Screen Door (🚌 20)

End LaurelThirst Public House (🚌 19)

Length 1.2 miles; seven hours

❶ Brave the brunch line

If you can actually get through the door at **Screen Door** (☎503-542-0880; www.screendoorrestaurant.com; 2337 E Burnside St; mains $9-15; ⏰8am-2pm & 5:30-10pm Mon-Fri, 9am-2:30pm & 5:30-10pm Sat, to 9pm Sun), you ought to feel accomplished. One of Portland's longest brunch lines is worth enduring for excellent plates of Southern-fried decadence. Fried chicken and waffles, biscuits and gravy, shrimp and grits, praline bacon waffles and more will stick to your ribs all day.

❷ Quirky gifts

Burn off brunch with a walk up NE 28th Ave to **ZimZim** (p115), a gift shop that sells items by independent makers. Peddling quirky apparel, hilarious tchotchkes and pop-culture novelties, it's a great place for souvenirs with local character, like a 'Straight Outta Portland' tee or a book on the city's best places to pee.

❸ Beer tasting

Continue up NE 28th Ave to NE Glisan St and take a right to **Migration Brewing** (p112). With reclaimed wood and galvanized steel fixtures, the casual-industrial atmosphere is an inviting space for a round of craft brews. Enjoy sports on the screens inside, or take a seat at one of the many outdoor tables if the weather permits.

❹ Wine time

From the brewery, take a left and continue down Glisan to **Pairings** (p115). Touting itself as a 'wine-geek-speak-free zone,' it takes pride in its designation as Portland's weirdest wine shop. It specializes in pairing wine with foods – but also with dog breeds, astrological signs and songs. Many of its bottles are organic, and it hosts events and classes.

❺ Munchies & mani-pedis

Situated along busy Sandy Blvd, the **Zipper** (www.facebook.com/thezipperpdx; 2705 NE Sandy Blvd; most dishes $6-12; ⏰11am-late; ☐12) is a modern food court in an architecturally intriguing space with plenty of outdoor seating. Look out for Basilisk, serving up one of Portland's best fried-chicken sandwiches. There's also a great nail salon called Finger Bang, open for late-night mani-pedis.

❻ Live tunes

Close out the evening with live music at the bustling **LaurelThirst Public House** (☎503-232-1504; www.laurelthirst.com; 2958 NE Glisan St; ⏰4pm-midnight Mon & Tue, to 1am Wed & Thu, to 2am Fri, 11am-2am Sat, 11am-midnight Sun). It's one of Portland's oldest independent live-music venues, hosting local acoustic acts mostly in the realm of bluegrass, folk and Americana. Most music is free nightly between 6pm and 8pm; later evening shows may have a small cover.

Explore

Southeast

Southeast Portland ranges from ultra-hip areas like Hawthorne to the up-and-coming like Foster-Powell. It swarms with busy street life and is replete with indie shops, acclaimed restaurants and fun bars. If that's not your scene, there are also some of the loveliest and most peaceful parks in the city.

The Short List

○ **Breweries (p112)** *Sampling craft suds at a range of tap houses like Hopworks Urban Brewery.*

○ **Top chef eats (p108)** *Making the rounds at numerous eateries helmed by Portland's culinary darlings, including Gabriel Rucker's Canard.*

○ **Doug Fir Lounge (p114)** *Catching touring and local indie bands in a subterranean venue with futuristic log-cabin decor.*

○ **Oregon Museum of Science & Industry (p108)** *Seeing science spring to life through interactive exhibits, lab demonstrations and a world-class planetarium.*

○ **Crystal Springs Rhododendron Garden (p108)** *Admiring a symphonic display of 2000 rhododendrons and azaleas at peak bloom.*

Getting There & Around

🚌 Routes 2, 12, 14, 15, 19 and 20 connect the city center with Southeast via its major thoroughfares.

🚃 The A Loop and B Loop streetcar lines connect with downtown via OMSI and Northeast via the convention center.

Neighborhood Map on p106

Crystal Springs Rhododendron Garden (p108)
TOMAS NEVESELY/SHUTTERSTOCK ©

Top Sight 📷
Craft Beer

Portland's 'Beervana' nickname is well earned, thanks to some 80 craft breweries in the city limits – more than anywhere in the world. The scene has been going strong since the 1980s, leaving beer lovers spoiled for choice. You can experience the best of Beervana in the Southeast quadrant's walkable neighborhoods, where great tasting rooms, brewpubs and bottle shops abound.

🚌 Southeast Portland is served by a number of routes; key ones include 2, 12, 14, 15, 19 and 20.

Blame it on the Water

Portland's fantastic craft beer begins with Oregon's delicious water, which is supplied by the Bull Run watershed in Mt Hood National Forest with rainfall, fog drip and snowmelt. Unspoiled forestland serves as a natural reservoir that absorbs, stores, filters and eventually releases water into pure streams. Unfiltered and unfluor-idated, the water supply is minimally treated before it flows from city taps.

Styles to Sample

In a beer landscape as saturated as Portland's, breweries must hustle to concoct brews that stand out. Expect to try anything from aggres-sive IPAs to ages-old European-style ales, and everything in between.

The city's most authentic English pub, Horse Brass (p113) pours from rare kegs and is the place for hand-pumped, cask-conditioned ales.

Cascade Brewing Barrel House (p112) is the city's prime pick for sour beers – you're guaran-teed to pucker up with any pour from its 28 taps.

Crafting especially unusual brews, Hair of the Dog Brewing (p112) uses a technique called 'bot-tle conditioning,' where several of its beers are re-fermented in the bottle. The result is a boost in alcohol content and complex flavor, as the beer continues to age like fine wine.

Brew-&-View Theaters

If you're torn between catching a movie or sampling microbrews, you can do both simultan-eously at Portland's 'brew-and-view' theaters. Southeast is home to some of the city's best, including the Hawthorne Theatre (p115), the Laurelhurst Theater (p114) and the Bagdad Theater (p114) – all wonderful, historic venues that screen a range of flicks to watch while you sip craft suds.

★ **Top Tips**

o Tasting rooms are a great way to sample several brews at once – but they're typically only open during the day and don't serve food, so plan accordingly.

o Though its neighborhoods are extremely walkable, Southeast is still an expansive area. Biking with a buzz isn't wise, so use the bus or a rideshare to get from district to district.

✕ **Take a Break**

With Southeast's many brewpubs, you can line your stomach and give your liver a break without having to change venues. Hopworks Urban Brewery (p112) has a vast selection of beer styles on tap to pair with its excellent food menu.

Walking Tour 🥾

The Best of Division-Clinton

Once a sleepy thoroughfare through a residential area, Division St has evolved into one of Portland's hippest drags over the last decade and is still rapidly developing. Several of the city's nationally acclaimed eateries and drinking establishments stretch along the main artery. Parallel and two blocks south, Clinton St features ultra-local hangouts nestled alongside beautiful modern and period homes.

Walk Facts

Start Broder (🚋 2, 4)
End Ava Gene's (🚋 2, 4)
Length 2 miles; six hours

❶ Scandi brunch

Begin the day at **Broder** (☎503-736-3333; www.broderpdx.com; 2508 SE Clinton St; mains $7-15; ⏱8am-3pm), a cozy neighborhood cafe on Clinton St with Scandinavian breakfast fare like fluffy egg scrambles. Breakfast boards feature house-cured gravlax, rye bread, cheese, beet-pickled hard-boiled eggs and granola parfaits. Finish with æbleskiver (crispy Danish pancake balls served with tart lemon curd and lingonberry jam).

❷ Spa indulgence

Let the Scandinavian theme continue with a trip to **Loyly** (☎503-236-6850; www.loyly.net; 2713 SE 21st Ave; 2hr sauna visit from $26; ⏱10am-9pm), a chic spa facility just off Clinton St with a cedar sauna and steam room. It offers spa and bodywork treatments such as Swedish massages and holistic facials, which you can bundle with sessions in the sauna.

❸ Daily bread

Make your way to **Little T American Baker** (☎503-238-3458; www.littletbaker.com; 2600 SE Division St; mains $6-9; ⏱7am-5pm Mon-Sat, 8am-2pm Sun) on Division St for a tea or java-based pick-me-up to prod you back into reality. Nosh on the best baguette in town, or grab a baked goodie like a pear Danish or chocolate-praline croissant to take and enjoy while you wait for the city's most famous chicken wings at your next stop.

❹ Pok Pok's signature wings

Among Division St's pioneering eateries is **Pok Pok** (p110), Portland's acclaimed Thai street food joint. James Beard Award–winning owner-chef Andy Ricker has drawn crowds with his fish-sauce wings since 2005. If you can't bear to wait in line (at least 20 minutes), Ricker's Whiskey Soda Lounge serves them, too – it's just across the street.

❺ Urban brews

Burn off lunch with a wander through the neighborhood to **Hopworks Urban Brewery** (p112) on Powell St. Admire the lovely arts-and-crafts homes as you walk south down SE 31st Ave, then cross over Powell St and take a right – the brewery will be on the left side. HUB specializes in all-organic beers; try the hazy or citrus IPAs.

❻ Save space for Italian

Award-winning trattoria **Ava Gene's** (☎971-229-0571; www.avagenes.com; 3377 SE Division St; mains $25-35; ⏱5-10pm Mon-Thu, to 11pm Fri, 4:30-11pm Sat, 4:30-10pm Sun) features a Roman-inspired menu that utilizes local, seasonal produce and Pacific Northwest–raised meats. Simple yet exceptional dishes include rustic vegetable plates with aromatic finishings and house-made pastas, which can also be served family-style. A creative cocktail menu and an extensive selection of Italian spirits round out an authentic experience. Reserve in advance!

Southeast

LLOYD

A 1

B

C

D

NE Lloyd Blvd

Banfield Expy

NE Oregon St · 16

NE Irving St

NE Glisan St

NE 22nd Ave

NE 24th Ave

· 36

Buckman
Field

NE Sandy Blvd

BUCKMAN

Burnside
Bridge

NE 9th Ave

NE 11th Ave

NE 12th Ave

18

NE Couch St

E Burnside St

7 8 28 25

17

SE Pine St

· 34

· 15

SE Stark St

E Burnside St

SE Ankeny St

SE Ankeny St

4

FH Steinbart Co

· 30

SE Stark St

SE 24th Ave

Lone Fir
Cemetery

Eastbank
Esplanade

2

SE Martin Luther King Jr Blvd

SE Grand Ave

Morrison
Bridge

3

SE Alder St

SE Morrison St

SE Belmont St

· 13

SE 12th Ave

· 24

SE Morrison St

Colonel
Summers
Park

21

SE Yamhill St

Hawthorne
Bridge

SE Water Ave

SE Sandy Blvd

SE 9th Ave

SE 11th Ave

SE 13th Ave

SE 15th Ave

SE 17th Ave

SE 19th Ave

SE Hawthorne Blvd · 6

4

Oregon Museum
of Science & Industry

3

SE Market St

SE 7th Ave

SE 8th Ave

SE 9th Ave

SE 11th Ave

SE 12th Ave

**LADD'S
ADDITION**

SE 20th Ave

SE 22nd Ave

SE 24th Ave

Marquam
Bridge

OMSI SE Water

**HOSFORD-
ABERNETHY**

5

Willamette
River

SE Grand Ave

SE McLoughlin Blvd

SE 8th Ave

SE 10th Ave

Clinton/SE
12th

SE Milwaukie Ave

SE Division St

SE Clinton St

SE 21st Ave

SE Powell Blvd

SE Pershing St

SE 17th
& Rhine

6

Ross
Island

Oaks Bottom
Wildlife Refuge

2 · · 31

BROOKLYN

A

B

C

D

Southeast

NORTH TABOR

MT TABOR

SUNNYSIDE

RICHMOND

Laurelhurst Park

Mazamas

Seawallcrest Park

Crystal Springs Rhododendron Garden

Creston Park

Banfield Expy

Oregon Park

NE 28th Ave
NE 31st Ave
NE 32nd Ave
NE 47th Ave
NE 39th Ave

NE Glisan St
NE Flanders St
NE Everett St
NE Couch St
E Burnside St

SE 28th Ave
SE 30th Ave
SE 32nd Ave
SE 33rd Ave
SE 34th Ave
SE Pine St
SE Stark St
SE Belmont St
SE Taylor St
SE Main St
SE Hawthorne Blvd

SE César E Chávez Blvd
SE Yamhill St
SE Salmon St
SE Clay St
SE Harrison St
SE Lincoln St
SE Sherman St
SE Division St

SE 43rd Ave
SE 47th Ave
SE 50th Ave

SE Belmont St

SE 26th Ave
SE 30th Ave
SE 32nd Pl
SE 34th Ave
SE 37th Ave
SE 38th Ave

SE Hawthorne Blvd

SE Division St
SE Clinton St
SE Woodward St
SE Franklin St

SE 31st Ave
SE 36th Ave

SE Powell Blvd

9
19
33
26
14
35
11
29
5
23
27
32
10
12
1
22

0   500 m
0   0.25 miles

For reviews see

◉	Sights	p108
❸	Eating	p108
⊖	Drinking	p111
✪	Entertainment	p114
🔒	Shopping	p115

Sights

Crystal Springs Rhododendron Garden

GARDENS

1 ⊙ MAP P106, E6

The large, beautiful grounds at this 5-acre garden near Reed College are covered with more than 2000 full-grown rhododendrons, azaleas and other plants, and there's a lagoon that's dotted with baby ducks in spring. Most of the garden is in bloom from late March or early April, peaking in May and continuing all summer. (📞503-771-8386; 5801 SE 28th Ave; Oct-Feb free, Mon free, Tue-Sun Mar-Sep $5; ⏱dawn-dusk; 🚹; 🚌19)

Oaks Bottom Wildlife Refuge

WILDLIFE RESERVE

2 ⊙ MAP P106, B6

Located in Sellwood, this large wetland of around 140 acres has a hiking trail through it, which connects with the nearby Springwater Corridor paved bike path. There's also good bird-watching – you can spot herons, egrets, hawks, osprey, hummingbirds, woodpeckers, falcons, vultures and more. (SE Sellwood Blvd & SE 7th Avenue)

Oregon Museum of Science & Industry

MUSEUM

3 ⊙ MAP P106, A4

This excellent museum offers hands-on science exhibits for kids, along with other temporary exhibits like 'The Science Behind Pixar.' There's also a movie theater, planetarium shows and a submarine tour (all carry a separate charge). Parking costs $5. (OMSI; 📞503-797-4000; www.omsi.edu; 1945 SE Water Ave; adult/child $14.50/10; ⏱9:30am-7pm Jun-Aug, to 5:30pm Tue-Sun Sep-May; 🚹; 🚌9, 17, 🚋A Loop, B Loop, 🚋Orange)

FH Steinbart Co

BREWING

4 ⊙ MAP P106, C2

This store offers beer-making classes, along with a great selection of home-brewing equipment. The basic brewing class ($30) is 2½ hours and includes a tasting. There are also regular free demonstrations at the store. Check class schedules online. (📞503-232-8793; www.fhsteinbart.com; 234 SE 12th Ave; classes from $30)

Mazamas

ADVENTURE SPORTS

5 ⊙ MAP P106, G2

Plug into the outdoor-adventure community with courses such as mountaineering, rock climbing and Nordic skiing, run by this educational organization. (📞503-227-2345; www.mazamas.org; 527 SE 43rd Ave; 8-week climbing course $525; ⏱office hours 11am-7pm Mon-Thu, 10am-2pm Fri)

Eating

Lardo

SANDWICHES $

6 🍴 MAP P106, C4

Definitely in the running for Portland's best sandwich, Lardo's take on Korean pork shoulder is outstanding – and that's on a menu of a dozen truly fantastic sandwiches. Try a guest-chef creation, different each month, and don't skip the addictive dirty fries, with Parmesan and pork scraps. (☎503-241-2490; www.lardosandwiches.com; 1212 SE Hawthorne Blvd; sandwiches $10-14; ⌚11am-10pm Sun-Thu, to 11pm Fri & Sat; ☐14)

Nong's Khao Man Gai   THAI $

7  MAP P106, B2

The widely adored food cart where it all started has closed, but Nong's brick-and-mortar locations still dish out her signature menu item: tender poached chicken with rice in a magical sauce. A handful of other options (including vegetarian) and add-ons are available, as well as occasional specials. (☎503-740-2907; www.khaomangai.com; 609 SE Ankeny St; mains $11-16; ⌚11am-9pm; ☐20)

Canard   FRENCH $$

8  MAP P106, B2

The hotly anticipated little sibling of chef Gabriel Rucker's rightly famous Le Pigeon (p111), Canard started winning 'best restaurant of the year' designations within weeks of opening at the start of 2018. With its wine-bar-meets-Parisian-brunch-cafe vibe, and a menu of mostly shareable dishes you won't find elsewhere, the place is a champ. (☎971-279-2356; www.canardpdx.com; 734 E Burnside St; dishes $6-20; ⌚8am-midnight Mon-Fri, from 9am Sat & Sun; ☐20)

Otters at Oaks Bottom Wildlife Refuge

Stammtisch

GERMAN $$

9 MAP P106, E1

Dig into serious German food – with a beer list to match – at this dark and cozy neighborhood pub. Don't miss the *Maultaschen* (a gorgeous pasta pocket filled with leek fondue in a bright, lemony wine sauce), the clams with *Landjäger* sausage in white wine broth, or the paprika-spiced roast chicken. (503-206-7983; www.stammtischpdx.com; 401 NE 28th Ave; small plates $5-9, mains $14-24; 3pm-1:30am Mon-Fri, 11am-1:30am Sat & Sun; 19)

Tasty n Daughters

AMERICAN $$

10 MAP P106, H5

After a nine-year run, chef John Gorham, of Toro Bravo (p92) fame, took brunch favorite Tasty n Sons, formerly on N Williams, to southeast Portland. The reboot – renamed to accurately reflect his offspring – retained favorites like *shakshuka* and *patatas bravas*, but added fresh pasta and seafood to the menu. Most notable is a new Turkish influence – the pide breakfast pizza is a must. (503-621-1400; www.tastyndaughters.com; 4537 SE Division St; small plates $3-14, mains $12-19; 9am-2:30pm & 5-10pm)

Ken's Artisan Pizza

PIZZA $$

11 MAP P106, E2

Glorious wood-fired, thin-crust pizzas with toppings such as pro-sciutto, fennel sausage and green garlic. Super-cool atmosphere, with huge sliding windows that open to the street on warm nights. Expect a long wait – no reservations taken. (503-517-9951; www.kensartisan.com; 304 SE 28th Ave; pizzas $13-18; 5-9:30pm Mon-Thu, 5-10pm Fri, 4-10pm Sat, 4-9pm Sun; 20)

Pok Pok

THAI $$

12 MAP P106, F5

Spicy Thai street food with a twist draws crowds of flavor-seekers to this famous eatery. Dishes are meant for sharing, so order lots and have fun. Don't miss the renowned chicken wings. To endure the wait, try a tastier-than-it-sounds drinking vinegar at the restaurant's bar, Whiskey Soda Lounge. (503-232-1387; www.pokpokpdx.com; 3226 SE Division St; mains $9-20; 11:30am-10pm)

Kachka

RUSSIAN $$

13 MAP P106, C3

There's a theme of homey nos-talgia at this Russian throwback restaurant, now in a new location and open for lunch as well as din-ner. *Babushka*-esque doilies and pastoral Russian artwork accent the experience here, and the food is mostly dumplings and hot or cold *zakuski* (appetizers tradition-ally washed down with vodka), with a Portland care to keeping ingredients local. (503-235-0059; www.kachkapdx.com; 960 SE 11th Ave; zakuski $8-14, mains $16-29; 11:30am-2pm & 4-10pm, to 11pm Fri & Sat; 15, 70)

Laurelhurst Market AMERICAN $$$

14 MAP P106, F2

Hugely popular and vegetarian-unfriendly is this hip and meaty spot, where grass-fed steaks, pork chops and free-range chicken dominate the menu. Just be prepared to wait, unless you have a reservation. There's also a butcher counter selling quality meats and great lunchtime sandwiches. (📞503-206-3097; www.laurelhurstmarket.com; 3155 E Burnside St; mains $17-54; ⏰5-10pm, butcher shop 10am-10pm)

Le Pigeon FRENCH $$$

Squeeze into this cozy, low-lit space next door to sister restaurant Canard (see 8 Map p106, B2) for some of Portland's best and most-loved cooking. Chef Gabriel Rucker does amazing things with meat and fish (but mostly meat) and whatever local produce is in season. The seven-course tasting menu ($105) is a complete experience. Sit at the bar to watch the action; most nights there'll be a wait for a table. (📞503-546-8796; www.lepigeon.com; 738 E Burnside St; mains $17-39; ⏰5-10pm; 🚌20)

Drinking

Push x Pull COFFEE

15 MAP P106, B2

A labor of love by a group of java-obsessed pals, this roastery and cafe specializes in natural-process coffees and offers a rotating selection of single-origins, plus local baked goods. Bright wood paneling and turquoise-painted walls that perfectly match the industrial schoolhouse furniture and espresso machines make for a cheery space – not to mention the delightfully friendly owners and staff. (www.pushxpullcoffee.com; 821 SE Stark St; ⏰7am-5pm Mon-Fri, 8am-4pm Sat & Sun)

Culmination Brewing MICROBREWERY

16 MAP P106, D1

At this comfortable tasting room in a refurbished old warehouse, you'll find some of the city's best beers (including the top-notch Phaedrus IPA plus a whole array of limited-edition seasonals) and a brief but unusually ambitious food menu. If the pêche is available, try it – even if you don't normally like 'fruit' beers. (📞971-254-9114; www.culminationbrewing.com; 2117 NE Oregon St; plates $5-16; ⏰noon-9pm Sun-Thu, to 10pm Fri & Sat; 🚌12)

Scotch Lodge COCKTAIL BAR

17 MAP P106, B2

Pouring some 300 international and domestic whiskeys in a cozy, subterranean space, Scotch Lodge certainly caters to connoisseurs – but its cocktails that blend whiskey with other spirits are creative and accessible, satisfying aficionado and noob alike. Try the 'Moneypenny' with dry gin, smoky Scotch and sea-bean-infused vermouth. Modern French-inspired bar bites like pumpernickel-battered fried Brie sticks are also available.

(☎503-208-2039; www.scotchlodge. com; 215 SE 9th Ave; ⏰4pm-midnight Wed-Sun)

Cider Riot BREWERY

18 🚋 MAP P106, B2

Portland's best cider company now has its very own pub and tasting room, so you can sample Everybody Pogo, Never Give an Inch or Plastic Paddy at the source. Ciders here are dry and complex, made with regional apples and hyper-regional attitude. (☎503-662-8275; www. ciderriot.com; 807 NE Couch St; ⏰4-11pm Mon-Fri, noon-11pm Sat, noon-9pm Sun; 🚌12, 19, 20)

Migration Brewing BREWERY

19 🚋 MAP P106, E1

Migration is a popular neighborhood brewpub with a great casual-industrial atmosphere. Wood picnic tables outside make it easy to see and be seen, and are especially wonderful on a warm day. There's good food, and sports fans will appreciate a Blazers or Timbers game on the screens inside. (☎503-206-5221; www.migrationbrewing. com; 2828 NE Glisan St; ⏰11am-11pm Mon-Sat, to 10pm Sun)

Cascade Brewing Barrel House BREWERY

20 🚋 MAP P106, B3

This excellent brewery specializes in sour beers, many made from fruit – which may leave some beer fiends skeptical, but trust us and give it a try. If you're hesitant, order

a few samplers (or just get the honey-ginger-lime). It all goes well with the gourmet food in the nice, big patio. (☎503-265-8603; www. cascadebrewingbarrelhouse.com; 939 SE Belmont St; ⏰noon-10pm Sun & Mon, to 11pm Tue-Thu, to midnight Fri & Sat)

Hair of the Dog Brewing BREWERY

21 🚋 MAP P106, A3

HOTD brews unusual beer styles, some of which are 'bottle-conditioned,' whereby the brewing cycle is finished inside the bottle. This results in complex flavors and high alcohol content, and the beer ages like a fine wine. Food is served to complement the beer's flavors. (☎503-232-6585; www.hairofthedog. com; 61 SE Yamhill St; ⏰11:30am-10pm Tue-Sat, to 8pm Sun; 🚌4, 6, 10, 14, 15, 🚋A Loop)

Hopworks Urban Brewery BREWERY

22 🚋 MAP P106, E6

All-organic beers made with local ingredients and served in an ecofriendly building with bicycle frames above the bar. Try the IPA or the Survival Stout, made with Stumptown coffee. There's a good selection of food and a family-friendly atmosphere, and the back deck can't be beat on a warm day. (HUB; ☎503-232-4677; www.hopworksbeer.com; 2944 SE Powell Blvd; ⏰11am-11pm Sun-Thu, to midnight Fri & Sat; 👪; 🚌9)

Horse Brass Pub

PUB

23  MAP P106, H3

Portland's most established English pub, cherished for its dark-wood atmosphere, excellent fish-and-chips and nearly 60 beers on tap. Also serves 'proper' 20oz imperial pints. Play some darts, watch soccer on TV and reminisce about the days when you couldn't see across the room through all the smoke. (503-232-2202; www.horsebrass.com; 4534 SE Belmont St; 11am-2:30am)

Crush

GAY

24  MAP P106, C3

Slip into this sexy lounge with all the pretty people, order one of the exotic cocktails and speak up – it gets loud, what with all the dancing and shows. Everyone is friendly and welcoming no matter what your leanings may be, and the cocktails and bar snacks are top-notch. (503-235-8150; www.crushbar.com; 1400 SE Morrison St; noon-2am, from 10am Sat & Sun)

Hey Love

COCKTAIL BAR

25  MAP P106, B2

Bright, colorful, high-octane craft cocktails and boozy, fruity frozen concoctions elicit perpetual summer vibes at this women-led lounge, attached to the Jupiter Next hotel. Rattan light fixtures, antique Moroccan carpets, thrift-store art and knick-knacks, and living plants suspended from the ceiling create a cozily eclectic atmosphere. A full menu of

Cascade Brewing Barrel House

internationally inspired dishes is served for lunch and dinner, plus weekend brunch. (☎503-206-6223; www.heylovepdx.com; 920 E Burnside St; ☽7am-2am)

Entertainment

Laurelhurst Theater   CINEMA

26 ★ MAP P106, E2

This great neighborhood theater has moved from showing second-run to mostly first-run movies, with occasional revival series. Pizza, salads, beer and wine are available; kids are welcome (with a parent) before 8pm. On Tuesday all tickets are matinee price. (☎503-232-5511; www.laurelhursttheater. com; 2735 E Burnside St; tickets $6.50-9; ☒20)

Bagdad Theater   CINEMA

27 ★ MAP P106, F4

This awesome, historic McMenamins venue offers microbrews on tap and pizza, burgers, salads and bar grub to go with its first-run films. (☎503-236-9234; www.bagdad movies.com; 3702 SE Hawthorne Blvd; adult/child under 12yr $10/7)

Doug Fir Lounge   LIVE MUSIC

28 ★ MAP P106, B2

Combining futuristic elements with a rustic log-cabin aesthetic, this venue has helped transform the LoBu (lower Burnside) neighborhood from seedy to slick. Doug Fir books great bands and the sound quality is usually tops. The attached restaurant offers a killer breakfast, weekend brunch and a bar menu ($8 to $13) until close. (☎503-231-9663; www.doug firlounge.com; 830 E Burnside St; ☽7am-2:30am; ☒20)

Goodfoot   LIVE MUSIC

29 ★ MAP P106, E2

Very neighborly spot with affordable music acts in the basement, plus good dancing (especially Friday nights) and a great sound system. Upstairs is a bar with booths, cheap pool tables, stiff drinks and creative art on the walls. Check out the open-mike night on Monday. (☎503-239-9292; www.thegoodfoot. com; 2845 SE Stark St)

Revolution Hall   CONCERT VENUE

30 ★ MAP P106, C2

Inside a remodeled 1924 school building (whose famous alumni include James Beard and Linus Pauling), this 850-seat concert venue has great sound quality and no bad seats. There's a rooftop bar with views toward downtown Assembly, a bar-lounge with 24 beers on tap; and two ground-floor cafe-bars, Martha's and the new Show Bar. (☎503-288-3895, tickets 877-435-9849; www.revolutionhall. com; 1300 SE Stark St; ☽box office 5-7pm; ☒15, 70)

Oaks Park   AMUSEMENT PARK

31 ★ MAP P106, C6

This amusement park in the is just run-down enough to be charming and kitschy, with fun rides, go-karts and a roller-skating rink.

The Hangar plays host to the **Rose City Rollers** (www.rosecity rollers.com; tickets from $15) roller derby team, whose showdowns are fast, furious and very entertaining. (📞503-233-5777; www.oakspark.com; 7805 SE Oaks Park Way)

Hawthorne Theatre   LIVE MUSIC

32 ⭐ MAP P106, G4

A good-sized, boxy venue inside a former Masonic Lodge, the Hawthorne Theatre is one of the few places in town that has an all-ages section. There's also a lounge that hosts more intimate gigs (21 years and over only). Check the calendar online for upcoming shows. (📞503-233-7100; www. hawthornetheatre.com; 1507 SE 39th Ave; 🚌14)

Shopping

ZimZim   GIFTS & SOUVENIRS

33 🅐 MAP P106, E1

An 'alternative' gift shop crammed with saucy birthday cards, badass-woman T-shirts and various other treasures (eg 'dumps for Trump' dog-poop bags, Mr Rogers lapel pins), this little corner store is a fun place to browse. You'll likely find something for that person you can otherwise never find a perfect present for. (📞503-235-0518; www. zimzimpdx.com; 144 NE 28th Ave; 🕐11am-7pm Mon-Sat, to 6pm Sun; 🚌19, 20)

Next Adventure   SPORTS & OUTDOORS

34 🅐 MAP P106, B2

This awesome outdoor store has plenty of sports clothing (including discounted items) and gear for hiking, camping, skiing and whatever else you have in mind. There's also a downstairs 'bargain basement' of used clothing and gear. (📞503-233-0706; www.nextadventure.net; 426 SE Grand Ave; 🕐10am-7pm Mon-Fri, to 6pm Sat, 11am-5pm Sun; 🚌6, 🚋A Loop, B Loop)

Music Millennium   MUSIC

35 🅐 MAP P106, F2

This place is a revelation with its extensive collections of everything from classic rock to straight-up classical. Check the listings of live in-store performances and grab a 'Keep Portland Weird!' sticker while you're here. (📞503-231-8926; www.musicmillennium.com; 3158 E Burnside St; 🕐10am-10pm Mon-Sat, 11am-9pm Sun)

Pairings   WINE

36 🅐 MAP P106, D1

This quirky wine shop pairs its products with rock songs, astrological signs and various moods (as well as more conventional food pairings). Most of the wines it sells are made from organically grown grapes. There are frequent classes and special events; check the website for details. (📞541-531-7653; www.pairingsportland.com; 455 NE 24th Ave; 🕐noon-10pm Mon-Sat, to 7pm Sun; 🚌12, 19, 20)

Worth a Trip 🔭
Columbia River Gorge

Driving east from Portland on I-84 (or on the scenic Historic Columbia River Hwy) has you passing high waterfalls and nearly vertical mountain walls that parallel the mighty Columbia. Hiking trails lead through fern-lined canyons and gushing rivers to grand vistas while wind sports, mountain biking and rafting opportunities abound. Wash the adventure down with wine, beer and cider tasting.

🚌 The Columbia Gorge Express service from Northeast Portland (Gateway) to Multnomah Falls ($2.50), Cascade Locks ($5) and Hood River ($7.50) allows you to visit the gorge for the day from Portland, without driving.

Columbia River Highway

Finished in 1915, the Historic Columbia River Hwy winds its scenic way between Troutdale and the Dalles. Also known as Hwy 30, the route offers access to waterfalls and awe-inspiring views all year round. Hwy 84 runs parallel and offers a much faster but less scenic route through the Columbia River Gorge.

From Portland, once you've passed Troutdale and entered the scenic area, you'll first come to a few viewpoints including the lovely (and often windy) **Vista House** (pictured; ☎503-344-1368; www.vistahouse.com; admission free; ⏱9am-4pm Oct-Apr, to 6pm May-Sep). The drive from here brings you to impressive waterfall after waterfall along the mossy, evergreen-clad roadside.

The tiny blue-collar town of Cascade Locks (at exit 44 off I-84; 44 miles from Portland) sits pretty on the Columbia River and you can visit the massive **Bonneville Dam** (☎541-374-8820; admission free; ⏱9am-5pm) nearby as well as Herman the (gigantic) sturgeon at the **Bonneville Fish Hatchery** (☎541-374-8393; 70543 NE Herman Loop; admission free; ⏱7am-5pm Nov-Feb, to 8pm Mar-Oct).

Hood River

The dynamic, gentrified town of Hood River (63 miles from Portland) is one of the best windsurfing and kiteboarding destinations in the world and attracts photogenic enthusiasts who zip back and forth across the wide Columbia River.

But Hood River offers more than awesome winds. The city has a bustling and pretty commercial core, with excellent shops, bars and restaurants lining a few steeply angled streets. In summer fruit stands and U-picks sell apples, pears, cherries, berries and vegetables. Premier wineries, breweries and cideries have also taken strong hold in the region.

★ **Top Tips**

○ The best views of the gorge are from Portland Women's Forum Park and Vista House.

○ Arrive before 9:30am to get parking at Multnomah Falls on weekends and sunny days.

✕ **Take a Break**

Eat at a Hood River brewery like **Ferment Brewing Company** (☎541-436-3499; www.fermentbrewing. com; 403 Portway Ave; beer/kombucha flights $10/7; ⏱11am-9pm Sun-Thu, to 10pm Fri & Sat).

For family-friendly grub on the riverside, don't miss **Thunder Island Brewing Co** (☎971-231-4599; www. thunderislandbrewing. com; 515 NW Portage Rd; mains $10-17, flights from $8; ⏱noon-8pm Mon-Wed, 11am-9pm Fri-Sun; 🚻🧒) in Cascade Locks.

Pick up some local smoked salmon for the road from Native American vendors under the Bridge of the Gods.

Consider taking a windsurfing or kiteboarding lesson – **Big Winds** (☎888-509-4210; www.bigwinds.com; 207 Front St; lessons $49; ⊘9am-5pm) is the biggest operator and is in downtown Hood River. It rents stand-up paddleboards too. Head south of town for great mountain biking. Most of the area's trails are off Hwy 35 and Forest Rd 44 (which branches off Hwy 35 about 20 miles south of Hood River). Good local rides include Post Canyon, Surveyor's Ridge and Nestor Peak. You can rent bikes at **Discover Bicycles** (☎541-386-4820; www.discoverbicycles.com; 210 State St; rentals per day $40-100; ⊘10am-6pm Mon-Sat, to 5pm Sun).

The Fruit Loop to Mt Hood

Covering 35 miles up Hwy 35, along scenic fertile lands and up a flank of Mt Hood, the Hood River County Fruit Loop takes you by family fruit stands, U-pick orchards, lavender fields, alpaca farms and winery tasting rooms. There are blossoms in spring, berries in summer, and apples and pears in fall – with plenty of festivals and celebrations through-out the seasons (except for winter). It's a good way to sample the area's agricultural bounties while appreciat-ing the local scenery too. Backtrack to Portland through the Gorge or drive over Mt Hood to Hwy 26 to add another hour to your drive. For more

Top Waterfalls

Waterfalls are at their gushiest in spring. The following are all off Hwy 30 (the Historic Columbia River Hwy), listed from west to east.

Bridal Veil Falls (140ft) Two-tiered falls reached via an easy half-mile walk. A separate wheelchair-accessible trail leads to great views.

Wahkeena Falls (242ft) Hike up the Wahkeena Trail, join Trail No 441 and head down to Multnomah Falls. Return via the road for the 4.8-mile loop.

Multnomah Falls (620ft) The gorge's top attraction. A 1-mile trail leads to the top. Continue up forested Multnomah Creek and the top of Larch Mountain (another 7 miles).

Horsetail Falls (176ft) Just east of Oneonta Gorge. A 2.6-mile loop begins here, passing through Ponytail Falls (and with an optional side trail to Triple Falls). Walk a half-mile east on Hwy 30 (passing the Oneonta Gorge) to return.

information and a list of events, check www.hoodriverfruitloop.com.

Easter Gorge & the Dalles

Located about 85 miles east of Portland, the Dalles features a decidedly different climate – much drier and sunnier. Though steadfastly unglamorous and down to earth (except for a few historic buildings), the city offers good outdoor recreation; there's decent camping and hiking, and fierce winds that are excellent for windsurfing and kiteboarding. The major stop here is the fun and educational **Columbia Gorge Discovery Center** (☎541-296-8600; www.gorgediscovery.org; 5000 Discovery Dr; adult/child $9/5; ☺9am-5pm) that covers the area's history from the floods that carved it to the Lewis and Clark expedition. For something a little more offbeat,

the new **National Neon Sign Museum** (☎541-370-2242; www.nationalneonsignmuseum.org; 20 East 3rd St; ☺10am-5pm Thu-Sat, reduced hours in winter; ♿) teaches you all about light bulbs and neon tubes.

East of The Dalles, the sights thin out a bit, and the landscapes turn from lush and mossy to windswept golden grass. It's a long drive to anywhere but there are some worthy places to check out, including the remarkable **Maryhill Museum of Art** (☎509-773-3733; www.maryhillmuseum.org; 35 Maryhill Museum Dr; adult/child $12/5; ☺10am-5pm mid-Mar–mid-Nov) and a replica of **Stonehenge** (US Hwy 97; admission free). Wine lovers should hit the brakes at **Maryhill Winery** (☎877-627-9445; www.maryhillwinery.com; 9774 Hwy 14; ☺noon-8pm Mon-Thu, to 9pm Fri & Sat, to 7pm Sun).

Willamette Valley Regions

Forest Grove ○
○ Portland

Gaston ○

McMinnville (p123)
The classic Americana downtown here is a great place to shop country-chic shops, dine and base yourself for a wine country adventure.

Newberg & Dundee (p133)
You'll find some exceptional dining and luxurious lodging in these small towns, that all pair great with tasting pinot noir at nearby wineries.

Salem (p141)
Visit the state capitol then head to nearby hot springs, a waterfall-filled state park and a Bavarian town topped with a Benedictine monastery.

Woodburn ○

○ Monmouth

Explore the Willamette Valley

The Willamette Valley is world famous for its fabulous and plentiful wineries, which could easily take several days to explore. They're not the region's only highlight, however. Visit humble Salem, Oregon's capital city, for its museums and stately buildings. Everything is so close by you'll want to linger for longer than you planned, so stretch that schedule and put on your explorer's hat – you'll need it.

Explore

McMinnville

At the heart of the region's wine industry lies busy and modern McMinnville, mostly charmless except for its historic, redbrick downtown district. Here you'll find art galleries, boutiques, wine-tasting rooms, fine restaurants and a few good hotels. The main regional attractions are the area's wineries, of course – many people opt to base themselves in McMinnville or nearby in order to explore the region.

The Short List

∘ **Wineries (p124)** Learning about the complexities of pinot noir in lovely, laid-back tasting rooms.

∘ **Dining (p130)** Sampling the exceptional locally driven menus at some of the most sought-after tables in the state.

∘ **Downtown McMinnville** Browsing scenic downtown's architecture, art galleries and adorable shops.

∘ **Evergreen Aviation & Space Museum (p128)** Getting geeky about airplanes then watersliding your cares away at the water park next door.

∘ **Festivals** Seeing the valley at its most lively during festivals like the International Pinot Noir Celebration and Wine Country Thanksgiving.

Getting There & Around

🚗 Renting a car is your best transport option. For chauffeured winery tours, check with the Chamber of Commerce.

🚌 Yamhill County Transit Area provides bus service around Yamhill County, with connections to Portland's MAX light-rail system and Salem.

McMinnville Map on p126

Over the Willamette Valley GREG VAUGHN/ALAMY STOCK PHOTO ©

Top Sight 📷
Wineries

Often considered the heart of the wine country, McMinnville and the surrounding areas are where the bulk of the Willamette Valley's wineries are located. Carlton, 7 miles north of McMinnville, and Dayton, 7 miles east, feature several vineyards, tasting rooms and retreats for oenophiles thirsty to sample Oregon's finest wines.

🚗 Designate a sober driver or hire a guide.

Oregon's Wine Bounty

Oregon's first wineries started up in the 1850s, but it wasn't until the late 1960s and early 1970s that the region's winemaking potential started to bear fruit. The northern Willamette Valley's mild climate and long summers foster the delicate pinot noir grape, as well as pinot gris, chardonnay and riesling.

Most vineyards are family-owned and welcome visitors to their tasting rooms, which range from grand edifices to homey affairs tucked into the corner of fermentation rooms. Before heading out to the wineries, double-check tasting-room hours (usually noon to 5pm Wednesday to Sunday, but some are open daily) and tasting fees ($10 to $20 for a flight).

Get a winery map at McMinnville's Chamber of Commerce, or see www.willamettewines. com, as there are more than 500 wineries in the region, and you'll want to narrow it down to two or three in a day. If the weather's nice, pack a lunch; wineries usually can't offer food, but many have picnic grounds.

If you're short of time, you don't have to visit the wineries to sip local wines. Some of the bigger wineries have tasting rooms in downtown Newberg, Dundee, Carlton or McMinnville. And there are always the region's restaurants, with their excellent wine lists.

Celebrate Grapes

Held in late July, the **International Pinot Noir Celebration** (pictured; www.ipnc.org; one-day pass $150; ☉Jul) is an important testing ground for pinot noir wines from all over the world. The three-day festival is immensely popular despite costing $1295 per person (including some meals); there's a public tasting on Sunday.

Wineries all across the Willamette Valley celebrate the **Thanksgiving holiday** (www. willamettewines.com; ☉Nov) with a weekend of special tastings, live music, food, tours and various other events.

★ Top Tips

○ Pop into the **Chamber of Commerce** (☎503-472-6196; www. mcminnville.org; 417 NW Adams St; ☉8am-5pm Mon-Fri) in McMinnville for maps, tips and information on wineries and other attractions in the area before you head out.

○ For the most relaxing approach, have a local tour operator drive you around. Good local choices include **Grape Escape** (☎503-283-3380; www.grapeescapetours. com; tours from $125), Oregon Select Wine Tours (p136) and Valley Vineyard Tours (p136).

✕ Take a Break

There's good eating in McMinnville, including some of the most sought-after tables in the state. Be sure to book ahead if you have your heart set on something.

For a break from all that wine, have a beer with lunch at Golden Valley Brewery (p131).

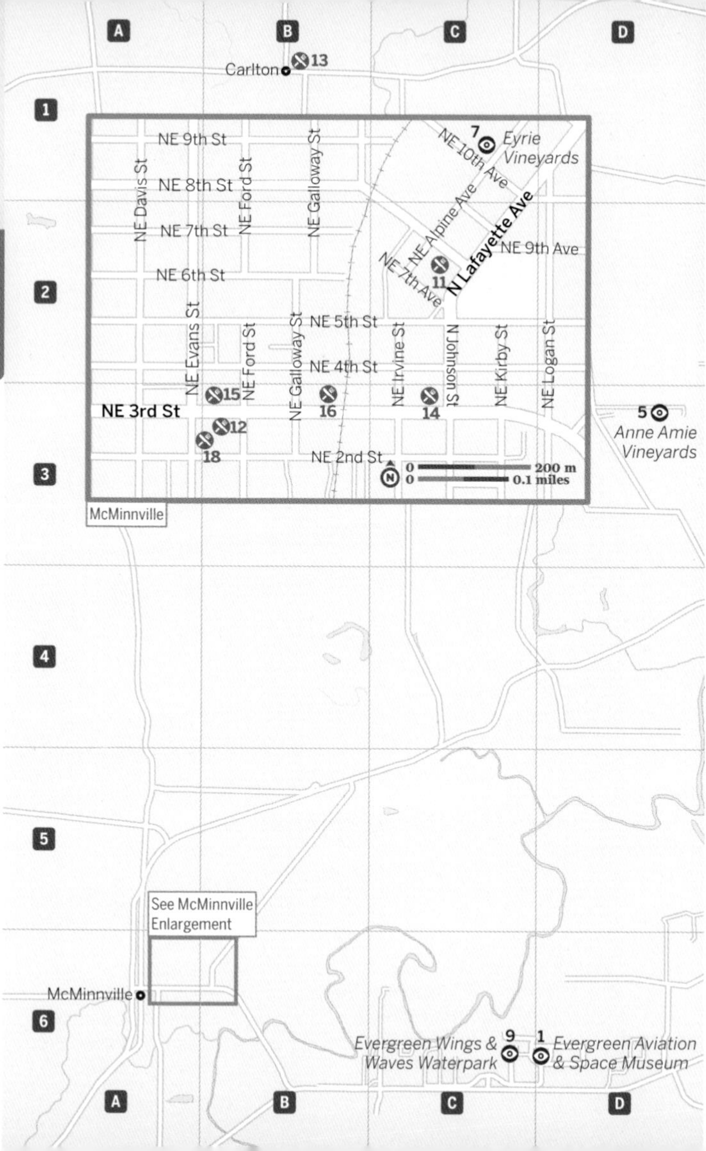

A B C D

Carlton ⊗13

1
NE 10th Ave
7 ⊙ Eyrie
Vineyards

NE 9th St

NE Davis St
NE 8th St
NE Ford St
NE 7th St
NE Galloway St

NE Alpine Ave
NE 9th Ave

N Lafayette Ave

NE 6th St

⊗11
NE 7th Ave

2

NE Evans St
NE Ford St
NE Galloway St
NE 5th St
NE Irvine St
N Johnson St
NE Kirby St
NE Logan St

NE 4th St

⊗15
NE 3rd St
⊗16
⊗14

5 ⊙
Anne Amie
Vineyards

⊗12
18

NE 2nd St
0   200 m
Ⓝ 0   0.1 miles

McMinnville

3

4

5

See McMinnville
Enlargement

McMinnville ●

6

Evergreen Wings & **9** ⊙ **1**
Waves Waterpark   Evergreen Aviation
& Space Museum

A B C D

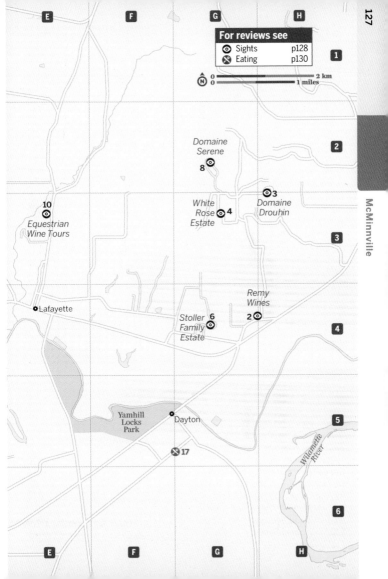

McMinnville

For reviews see
👁 Sights   p128
✖ Eating   p130

Ⓝ 0 ————————— 2 km
    0 ————————— 1 miles

Domaine
Serene
8 👁

👁3
White   Domaine
Rose 👁4   Drouhin
Estate

10 👁
Equestrian
Wine Tours

Remy
Wines
Stoller 6   2 👁
Family 👁
Estate

● Lafayette

Yamhill
Locks
Park   ● Dayton

✖17

Willamette River

Sights

Evergreen Aviation & Space Museum

MUSEUM

1 ◎ MAP P126, D6

A mile east of McMinnville, this museum showcases Howard Hughes' *Spruce Goose,* the world's largest wood-framed airplane. In 1947, with Hughes at the wheel, the airplane flew for just under a mile – and never took off again. Plenty of other aircraft are on display, including propeller planes, small jets, fighters, biplanes and helicopters. A different building offers excellent space-exploration exhibits. There's also a 3-D digital theater, along with two cafes and gift shops. Tours are available. (☏503-434-4180; www.evergreenmuseum.org; 500 NE Captain Michael King Smith Way; adult/child $19/27; ◷9am-5pm; ♿)

Remy Wines

WINE

2 ◎ MAP P126, G4

In a landscape known for French heritage wines, Remy Drabkin brings old world Italy to the Willamette Valley. Specializing in single-vineyard, single-varietal Italian wines, Remy's craft isn't the only unique thing about her – she could be the only Jewish lesbian winemaker in Oregon. Sip sangiovese or dolcetto at the rustic tasting room set in a historic farmhouse in the Dundee foothills. (☏503-864-8777; www.remywines.com; 17495 NE McDougall Rd; flights $10-15; ◷noon-5pm)

Domaine Drouhin

WINE

3 ◎ MAP P126, H3

For grand atmosphere and panoramic views, plus well-established pinot and chardonnay from the surrounding Dundee Hills, stop in at Domaine Drouhin. (☏503-864-2700; www.domainedrouhin.com; 6750 NE Breymen Orchards Rd; flights $20; ◷11am-4pm)

White Rose Estate

WINE

4 ◎ MAP P126, G3

Set atop a hill with sweeping views of surrounding vineyards, White Rose is heralded for pinot noirs made in a 'neoclassical' style – a modern approach to historical, whole-cluster fermentation. Built into the hill and over the cellar, the chilly, windowless tasting room still manages to elicit an inviting warmth, thanks in large part to the cheery and knowledgeable manager, Dago Guillén. (☏503-864-2328; www.whiteroseestate.com; 6250 NE Hilltop Lane; tastings $25; ◷11am-5pm)

Anne Amie Vineyards

WINE

5 ◎ MAP P126, D3

You'll find some very distinctive pinot noirs and zero pretentiousness at this fun and friendly tasting room located just outside Carlton. The reserve pinot noir and sparkling rosé are top notch, and for those after something a little different there's also a dessert wine on offer. (☏503-864-2991; www.anneamie.com; 6580 NE Mineral

Springs Rd; flights $15; ⊘10am-
4:45pm daily Mar-Dec, Thu-Mon only
Jan & Feb)

Stoller Family Estate   WINE

6 ⊙ MAP P126, G4

The world's first LEED Gold–
certified winery, Stoller is as
impressive as it is easy to reach.
The 4000-sq-ft tasting room is
well worth checking out, even
for non-enthusiasts. (☑503-864-
3404; www.stollerfamilyestate.com;
16161 NE McDougall Rd; flights $20;
⊘11am-5pm)

Eyrie Vineyards   WINE

7 ⊙ MAP P126, C1

Eyrie is home to the first pinot
noir and chardonnay plantings

in the Willamette Valley, and the
first pinot gris plantings in the US.
Find the remodeled tasting room
in McMinnville, open by appointment Thursday through Monday,
with seatings at 11am and 2pm.
(☑503-472-6315; www.eyrievineyards.
com; 935 NE 10th Ave; tastings $40;
⊘tastings by appointment only, 11am
& 2pm Thu-Mon)

Domaine Serene   WINE

8 ⊙ MAP P126, G2

Try the rosé or the signature pinot
noirs amid stunning views at this
hilltop vineyard. (☑503-864-4600;
www.domaineserene.com; 6555 NE
Hilltop Lane; tasting fee $25; ⊘tast-
ing room 11am-4pm Mon-Thu, to 5pm
Fri-Sun)

Evergreen Aviation & Space Museum

Evergreen Wings & Waves Waterpark
WATER PARK

9 MAP P126, C6

A must on a hot day, this indoor water park is next to the aviation museum (p128) and quite unmissable – a retired Boeing 747 lies atop the building. Inside are 10 waterslides (including four that come out of the 747), a wave pool, a splashing play structure, a leisure pool and a bubbly toddler area. Plenty of lifeguards keep everyone safe. (📞503-687-3390; https://wingsandwaveswaterpark.com; 500 NE Captain Michael King Smith Way; visitors under/over 42in $20/29, dry passes $10; ⏱10am-6pm or 7pm, varies with season; 👪)

Equestrian Wine Tours
WINE

10 MAP P126, E3

Tour the Red Hills around Dundee on horseback or by carriage, stopping at various winery tasting rooms. Minimal risk of a DUI! Tours depart from Winter's Hill Estate (www.wintershillwine.com) in Dayton. (📞503-864-2336; www.equestrianwinetours.com; 6325 NE Abbey Rd; 2.5hr tour per person $190)

Eating

Valley Commissary
AMERICAN $

11 MAP P126, C2

Bolster your belly before wine tasting at this breezy, elevated daytime joint. For breakfast and brunch, try the pulled pork, egg and sweet potato burrito, or chicken and waffles with fried sage and hot sauce butter. Come noon, opt for the pork-belly sandwich with house-made kimchi, a chickpea burger with smoked lime yogurt, or the spring veggie grilled cheese. (📞503-883-9177; 920 NE 8th St; mains $8-15; ⏱7am-3pm Mon-Fri, brunch 9am-3pm Sat & Sun; 🎵)

Crescent Cafe
AMERICAN $$

12 MAP P126, B3

Solid breakfast spot serving up comfort dishes like creamed chicken and biscuits with eggs, or a grilled ham and cheddar sandwich with caramelized onions. Try the passion-fruit bellini and apple cinnamon crepes or a classic Reuben sandwich for lunch. Expect a long wait on weekends. (📞503-435-2655; www.crescentcafeonthird.com; 526 NE 3rd St; breakfast mains $6-14; ⏱7am-2pm Wed-Fri, from 8am Sat & Sun)

The Horse Radish
AMERICAN $$

13 MAP P126, B1

Gourmet meals, cheese plates and a wine bar in the heart of Carlton, with weekly dinner specials (6pm to 8pm Friday and Saturday) featuring dishes like BBQ shrimp and cheddar grits, or green chili-stuffed chicken breasts with black beans and rice. There's live music on Friday and Saturday nights. (📞503-852-6656; www.thehorseradish.com; 211 W Main St; small-plate combos $12-18; ⏱noon-3pm Sun-Thu, to 10pm Fri & Sat)

Golden Valley Brewery

AMERICAN $$

14 🍴 MAP P126, C3

This top-notch brewery-restaurant offers great small plates, salads and sandwiches, along with gourmet burgers and steaks – made with meat from its own ranch. (📞503-472-2739; www.goldenvalleybrewery. com; 980 NE 4th St; mains $9-25; 🕙11am-10pm Mon-Thu, to 11pm Fri & Sat, to 9pm Sun)

Nick's Italian Cafe

ITALIAN $$

15 🍴 MAP P126, B3

Going strong for over 30 years, Nick's was named one of 'America's Classics' by the James Beard Foundation in 2014. It doesn't offer slick, contemporary decor, but it does have timeless Italian cuisine. There's also excellent wood-fired pizza and great appetizers. (📞503-434-4471; www.nicksitaliancafe.com; 521 NE 3rd St; pizzas $15-17, mains $16-29; 🕙5-9pm Thu-Tue)

Bistro Maison

FRENCH $$$

16 🍴 MAP P126, B3

This European eatery is one of McMinnville's, and the region's, best restaurants, serving up exceptional French dishes like duck confit, *cassoulet* (casserole with meat and white beans) and *coq au vin* (chicken braised in red wine). Try the croque monsieur or madame for lunch (mains $14 to $19). The lovely garden patio is mandatory on warm summer nights.

(📞503-474-1888; www.bistromaison. com; 729 NE 3rd St; mains $28-38; 🕙5:30-9pm Wed-Sat, noon-7pm Sun)

Joel Palmer House

NORTHWESTERN US $$$

17 🍴 MAP P126, G5

Renowned for its dishes built around wild mushrooms and Oregon truffles (often handpicked by the chef, Christopher Czarnecki), this highly lauded restaurant is just a few miles northwest of McMinnville, in Dayton. It's one of Oregon's finest eateries, turning local ingredients into unforgettable fine cuisine. Reservations recommended. (📞503-864-2995; www.joelpalmerhouse.com; 600 Ferry St; 3-course menu from $65; 🕙4:30-9:30pm Tue-Sat)

Thistle

NORTHWESTERN US $$$

18 🍴 MAP P126, B3

Small but top-drawer restaurant run by Eric Bechard, an award-winning chef who fiercely believes in using local, organic ingredients whenever possible. The menu changes daily and is posted on a chalkboard, and while portions are small they are well created and truly delicious. If you're having decision fatigue after a long day, your table can opt for the 'Chef's Whim.' (📞503-472-9623; www.thistlerestaurant.com; 228 NE Evans St; mains $24-27; 🕙5:30-9pm Tue-Sat)

Explore

Newberg & Dundee

The gateways to wine country, these small cities, just a couple of miles apart, were originally founded as Quaker settlements. These days, car traffic, strip malls and modern services are much of what you'll see. There are excellent restaurants here, however, along with upscale places to sleep.

The Short List

○ **Wine tasting (p136)** *Sampling the best pinots of the region at wineries and tasting rooms spread in and around these towns.*

○ **Champoeg State Heritage Area (p137)** *Taking a break from wine to explore serene woodlands and riverbanks and learn about Oregon history.*

○ **Dining (p137)** *Delighting in the good food around here, from picnic supplies to fine dining.*

○ **Shopping (p139)** *Heading into an adorable shop like Velour to go vintage Pacific Northwest to handmade country-chic.*

Getting There & Around

Dundee is 2 miles west of Newberg, on Hwy 99W.

🚗 Renting a car is the best way to get around. Numerous wine tours are also available.

🚐 Caravan Shuttle provides shuttle services to/from Portland's airport ($42 one-way per person).

Newberg & Dundee Map on p134

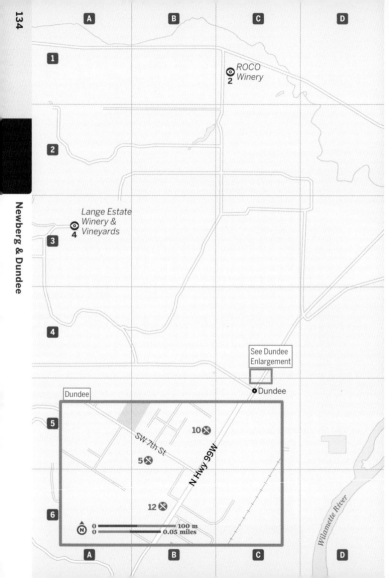

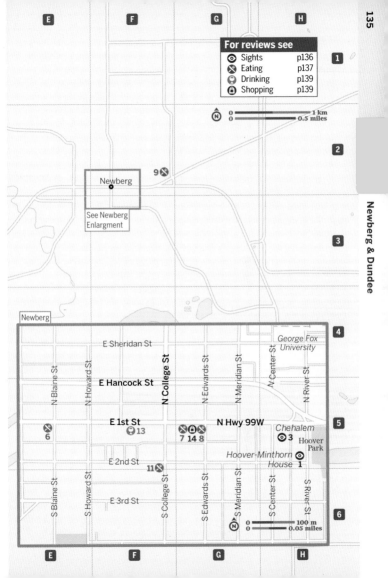

For reviews see

◉	Sights	p136
✖	Eating	p137
🍷	Drinking	p139
🛍	Shopping	p139

0 — 1 km
0 — 0.5 miles

Newberg

See Newberg
Enlargement

9 ✖

Newberg

E Sheridan St

George Fox
University

E Hancock St

E 1st St
🍷 13

N Hwy 99W

✖◉🛍✖
7 14 8

Chehalem
◉ 3

Hoover
Park

✖
6

Hoover-Minthorn ◉
House 1

E 2nd St
11 ✖

E 3rd St

0 — 100 m
0 — 0.05 miles

S Blaine St
N Blaine St
N Howard St
S Howard St
N College St
S College St
N Edwards St
S Edwards St
N Meridian St
S Meridian St
N Center St
S Center St
N River St
S River St

Sights

Hoover-Minthorn House

MUSEUM

1 ⊙ MAP P134, H5

This house is where Herbert Hoover (the 31st president of the USA) grew up. Built in 1881, the restored home is now a museum of period furnishings and early Oregon history. Call ahead outside summer; hours vary, but appointments are possible during off season. (☎503-538-6629; www. hooverminthorn.org; 115 S River St; adult/child $5/free; ☺1-4pm Wed-Sun Mar-Oct, closed Jan, limited hours rest of year)

ROCO Winery

WINE

2 ⊙ MAP P134, C1

Named after its delightful owners, Rollin and Corby Soles, ROCO specializes in small-production pinot noir, chardonnay and sparkling wines. Rollin, co-founder and former head winemaker at **Argyle Winery** (☎503-538-8520; www.argylewinery.com; 691 Hwy 99W; flights $20; ☺11am-5pm Mon-Thu, from 10am Fri-Sun), has been a pioneer of Oregon sparkling wine for more than 30 years. The newly released 2016 RMS Brut Rosé is a particular standout, best enjoyed on the cozy tasting room's zen-garden patio. (☎503-538-7625; www.rocowinery.com; 13260 NE Red Hills Rd; tasting flights $15-20; ☺11am-5pm)

Oregon Select Wine Tours

WINE

Focusing on boutique wineries around Newberg, Dundee and McMinnville, Oregon Select Wine Tours provides custom tours in full-size luxury SUVs. The hourly rate is for up to six people; ask about larger groups. Add a gourmet picnic lunch or charcuterie plate for an additional fee. (☎971-404-5178; www.oregonselectwinetours.com; tour per hour $75)

Valley Vineyard Tours

WINE

This Newberg-based operation provides laid-back, custom wine country tours for up to six passengers ($100 per hour for more than six). Can also arrange airport transfers to and from Newberg ($110). (☎971-267-5444; www.valley vineyardtours.com; tour per hour $75)

Chehalem

WINE

3 ⊙ MAP P134, H5

Private tastings at the winery; public tastings at its Newberg tasting room. There's also wine on tap at the tasting room, where you can fill up a keepsake glass bottle. (☎503-538-4700; www. chehalemwines.com; 106 S Center St; flights $20; ☺11am-5pm Sun-Thu, to 8pm Fri & Sat)

Lange Estate Winery & Vineyards

WINE

4 ⊙ MAP P134, A3

Family-run Lange is known for good-value, single-vineyard pinot noir. The grounds have gorgeous views and shaggy dogs running around. (📞503-538-6476; www.langewinery.com; 18380 NE Buena Vista Dr; tastings from $15; 🕙11am-5pm)

Eating

Red Hills Market
AMERICAN $

5 MAP P134, B5

This deli-market offers a great atmosphere, with its wines and gourmet food products surrounding a small cluster of diners in the main room. Head to the excellent back patio to enjoy your toasted, open-faced 'craft' sandwich, made from fancy charcuterie, or a (semi) healthy breakfast bowl. A few salads and wood-fired pizzas are also available. (📞971-832-8414; www. redhillsmarket.com; 155 SW 7th St; mains $7-18; 🕙7am-8pm)

Storrs Smokehouse
BARBECUE $

6 MAP P134, E5

The folks behind the upscale Painted Lady (p138) have taken their genius down home with this Southern-style barbecue joint. Brisket, pulled pork, ribs and wings are smoked for days, resulting in slip-off-the-bone tenderness and deep flavor. Can't pick a protein? Try them all with the Grandaddy platter. Slather everything in their homemade Oregon Pinot Noir BBQ sauce. Let meat coma ensue. (📞503-538-8080; www.storrssmokehouse.com; 310 E 1st St; meat plates $8-19; 🕙8am-8pm Wed-Sun)

Champoeg State Heritage Area

A state heritage area and popular family destination, **Champoeg** (📞503-678-1251; www.oregonstateparks.org; 7679 Champoeg Rd NE; day fee $5; 🕙10am-4:30pm; 🚼) is 25 miles southwest of Portland and 6 miles southeast of Newberg. There are 615 acres of old-growth woodland, grassy meadows, nature trails, historic sites, campgrounds and a playground. Films and displays at the visitor center explain the events that led up to the famous vote, in 1843, that formed the Northwest's first provisional government.

Rosmarino Osteria Italiana
ITALIAN $$

7 MAP P134, G5

Originally from outside of Milan, chef Dario Pisoni prepares simple and delicious northern Italian dishes based on recipes inherited from his *nonna* (grandmother). Key ingredients like olive oil, cheese, flour and Carnaroli rice are all imported from his native home, and you can expect classics like hearty braised meats and risotto on the weekly changing menu. Reservations essential. (📞503-438-6211; www.osteriarosmarino.com; 714 E 1st St; lunch mains $8-15, five-course tasting menu $95; 🕙11:30am-2:30pm & 5:30-8pm Thu, 11:30am-2:30pm &

6:30-8pm Fri, 11:30am-2:30pm & 6:30-9pm Sat, 11:30am-7:30pm Sun & Mon)

Ruddick/Wood
AMERICAN $$

8 MAP P134, G5

Set in a converted 1920s garage, this classy yet casual restaurant and tavern has perfected local, seasonal new-American fare. The open kitchen, encircled by a copper-top bar with seating, cranks out small plates like duck and oat hushpuppies and crispy Dungeness crab and shrimp cakes. Heartier mains include chicken roulade and mushroom and shell bean falafel with cauliflower couscous. (503-487-6133; www.ruddickwood.com; 720 E 1st St; dinner mains $13-28; 11:30am-10:30pm Tue-Thu, to 11:30pm Fri, 10am-11:30pm Sat, 10am-10:30pm Sun)

Newbergundian Bistro
BISTRO $$

9 MAP P134, F2

This cozy bistro with an open kitchen serves up American classics like burgers, a wedge salad and oysters Rockefeller, plus European-inspired fare. Bouillabaisse with shrimp, mussels and halibut, crispy polenta with hazelnut pesto, and a croque monsieur with smoked ham hock are all expertly executed. The service is swift and cheery. (971-832-8687; www.newbergundian.com; 203 Villa Rd; dinner mains $11-26; 11am-10pm Mon, Wed, Thu & Sun, to 11pm Fri & Sat)

Dundee Bistro
NORTHWESTERN US $$

10 MAP P134, B5

This modern, popular restaurant is owned by Ponzi Vineyards and has a wine-tasting room next door. Dishes like Oregon Ling cod and chips, or pappardelle pasta with braised wild boar grace the menu, which changes seasonally. The gourmet pizza offers a more casual option. On warm days go for the great back patio. (503-554-1650; www.dundeebistro.com; 100 SW 7th St; mains $16-32; 11:30am-9pm)

Painted Lady
NORTHWESTERN US $$$

11 MAP P134, F5

Accomplished chefs Allen Routt and Jessica Bagley use their wide travel and culinary experiences at this renowned restaurant in a renovated 1890s Victorian house. The multicourse set menus include choices of appetizer, like Dungeness crab with miso custard, mains like dry-aged New York strip steaks with pea puree, and desserts like honey lavender mousse, with the option of a wine pairing. (503-538-3850; www.thepaintedladyrestaurant.com; 201 S College St; prix fixe $95-110; 5-10pm Wed-Sun)

Tina's
NORTHWESTERN US $$$

12 MAP P134, B6

This small, renowned French-influenced restaurant does meat dishes such as lamb, rabbit and duck to perfection. Expect local, organic and seasonal ingredients, and a killer wine list. Reservations recommended. (📞503-538-8880; www.tinasdundee.com; 760 Hwy 99W; mains $29-46; ⏱5-9pm)

Drinking

Bar Deux

BAR

13 🚇 MAP P134, F5

Rowdy nightlife is nil in Newberg, but if you're after a casual tipple, saddle up to the reclaimed wood bar at this cozy, hyperlocal watering hole. The wine list is both regional and global, and cocktails run the gamut from classics to seasonally inspired handcrafts with fresh juices and top-shelf spirits. Elevated shared plates like Wagyu steak tartare and handmade pasta (📞503-487-6853; www.

bardeuxnewberg.com; 602 E 1st St; ⏱5-9pm Tue-Sat)

Shopping

Velour

VINTAGE

14 🔒 MAP P134, G5

Americana folk meets Pacific Northwest heritage at Velour, an aesthetic-forward lifestyle shop curating vintage and handmade clothing, jewelry and accessories, plus a selection of small homewares. Think vintage Danner hiking boots, canvas military backpacks, voile lace dresses, '70s band tees, rattan baskets and a healthy selection of buffalo plaid. Quality and artisanship are standard, no matter what you score. (📞503-718-8118; www.shopvelour.com; 716 E 1st St; ⏱11am-6pm Mon-Sat)

Newberg & Dundee Drinking

Red Hills Market (p137)

Explore ◉

Salem

The state capital is a peaceful university city that makes a good day trip from Portland, as it's just an hour's drive south. Highlights include the state capitol and a few museums, along with a riverfront park complete with carousel. Outside the city limits are more interesting destinations, including a spectacular state park, a hilltop abbey and a beautiful themed garden.

The Short List

○ **Trail of Ten Falls Loop (p144)** *Hiking this sublime trail in Silver Falls State Park – and walking behind waterfalls.*

○ **Breitenbush Hot Springs (p146)** *Soaking your tired muscles in the healing waters.*

○ **Oregon Garden (p144)** *Exploring 80 acres of varied and gorgeous gardens on foot or by tram.*

○ **Mount Angel (p145)** *Taking in this Bavarian-style town with a tranquil hilltop abbey and a rocking Oktoberfest.*

○ **Oregon State Capitol (p146)** *Getting to the heart of the state of Oregon by touring this art deco building.*

Getting There & Around

🚆 Trains to/from Portland ($16, 1½ hours, nine daily) stop at the Amtrak station.

🚌 Greyhound services also depart from the Amtrak station for Portland ($14, one hour, four daily).

Salem Map on p142

Oregon State Capitol building, and Capitol Fountain by Weltzin B Blix, sculptor BOB POOL/SHUTTERSTOCK ©

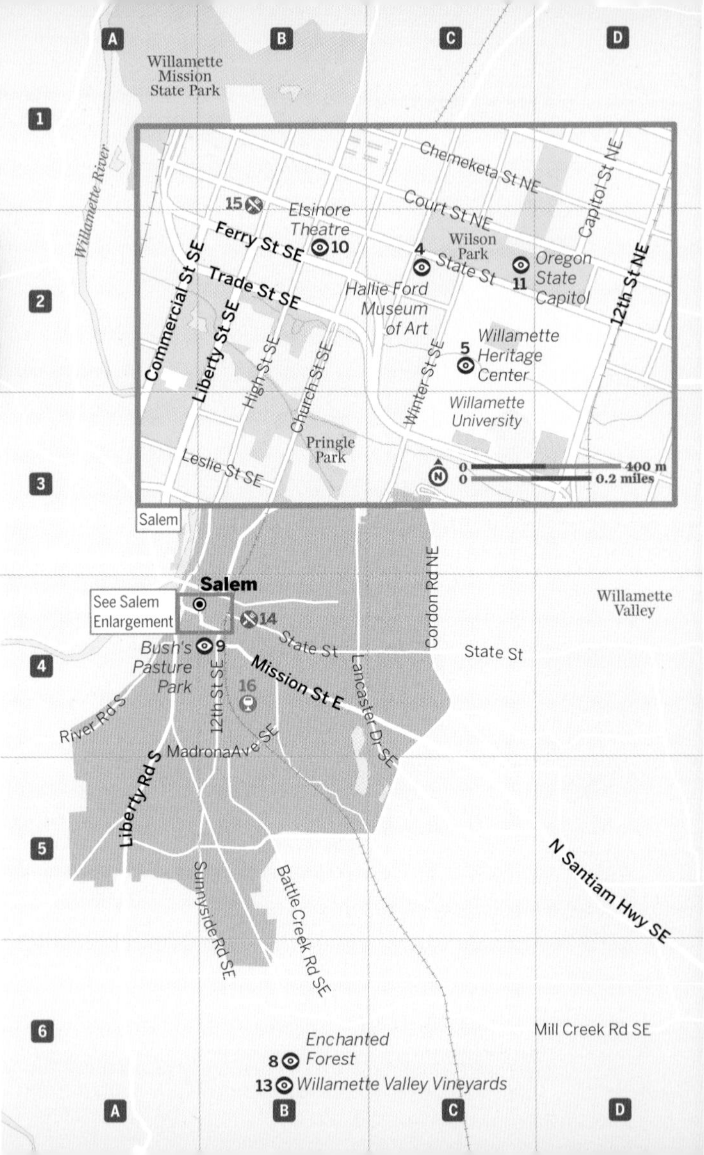

Salem

A
B
C
D

Willamette Mission State Park

Willamette River

1

Chemeketa St NE

Court St NE

Capitol St NE

15 ⊗
Elsinore Theatre

Ferry St SE

⊙10

Wilson Park

4 ⊙
State St

11 ⊙
Oregon State Capitol

2

Commercial St SE

Liberty St SE

Trade St SE

High St SE

Church St SE

Hallie Ford Museum of Art

Winter St SE

5 ⊙
Willamette Heritage Center

12th St NE

Willamette University

Leslie St SE

Pringle Park

Salem

0 ———— 400 m
Ⓝ 0 ———— 0.2 miles

3

Salem
⊙

See Salem Enlargement

⊗14

State St

Cordon Rd NE

Willamette Valley

Bush's ⊙9
Pasture Park

Mission St E

State St

4

River Rd S

16 Ⓗ

12th St SE

Lancaster Dr SE

Madrona Ave

Liberty Rd S

5

Sunnyside Rd SE

Battle Creek Rd SE

N Santiam Hwy SE

6

Enchanted
8 ⊙ Forest

13 ⊙ Willamette Valley Vineyards

Mill Creek Rd SE

A
B
C
D

E

Mount Angel ⊙7
Fisher Memorial Park

F

🍴17 ⊙ **Mount Angel** 6 *Abbey*

G

H

For reviews see

⊙ Sights   p144
✗ Eating   p146
🍴 Drinking   p147

Ⓝ 0 ————————————— 5 km
     0 ————————————— 2.5 miles

1

Silverton ●   Cascade Hwy NE

2

3 *Gordon House* ⊙
2 ⊙
Oregon Garden

Cascade Hwy NE

3

Silver Falls Dr NE

4

Silver Falls State Park

Silver Falls 1 5
State Park ⊙

Cascade Hwy SE

Silver Falls Hwy SE

6

S Center St

Breitenbush Hot Springs
12 ⊙▲

E   F   G   H

Sights

Silver Falls State Park

PARK

1 ◉ MAP P142, H5

Oregon's largest state park, Silver Falls, located 26 miles east of Salem on Hwy 214, is an easy day trip from Portland, Salem and Eugene. It offers camping, swimming, picnicking, cycling and horseback riding. Best of all are the hikes, the most famous being the **Trail of Ten Falls Loop**, a relatively easy 8-mile loop that winds up a basalt canyon through thick forests filled with ferns, moss and wildflowers. (☎503-873-8681; www. oregonstateparks.org; day fee $5, tent sites/RV sites/cabins $19/29/43)

Oregon Garden

GARDENS

2 ◉ MAP P142, F2

Plant lovers shouldn't miss this garden, located 15 miles east of Salem outside Silverton. Over 20 specialty gardens are showcased on 80 acres, including a Northwest plant collection, miniature conifer section, children's garden and even a pet-friendly garden. There are 5 miles of walking trails, with a tram that runs on weekends for those with mobility issues. Be sure to check the website for events like classes and lectures. Opening hours and admission prices vary year-round. (☎503-874-8100; www.oregongarden.org; 879 W Main St; adult/student $14/8; ◷9am-6pm)

Gordon House

HISTORIC SITE

3 ◉ MAP P142, F2

Next to the Oregon Garden in Silverton is the Gordon House, the only building in Oregon designed by Frank Lloyd Wright. It was built in 1964 and moved to its present location in 2002. Opening hours and days vary; reservations essential, book ahead online. (☎503-874-6006; www.thegordonhouse.org; 869 W Main St; tours $20; ◷tours noon, 1pm & 2pm)

Hallie Ford Museum of Art

MUSEUM

4 ◉ MAP P142, C2

Willamette University's Hallie Ford Museum of Art boasts the state's best collection of Pacific Northwest art, including an impressive Native American gallery. (☎503-370-6855; www.willamette.edu/arts/hfma; 700 State St; adult/child $6/free, Tue free; ◷10am-5pm Tue-Sat, 1-5pm Sun)

Willamette Heritage Center

MUSEUM

5 ◉ MAP P142, C2

This interesting 5-acre complex houses grassy gardens, two gift shops, a clutch of pioneer buildings and two museums. The Mission Mill Museum, Jason Lee House (1841), John Boon House (1847), Methodist Parsonage (1841) and an old Presbyterian church (1858) all look pretty much as they did in the 1840s and 1850s. The Thomas Kay Woolen Mill was built in 1889 and was powered by a mill race (waterway), a section of which still runs through the grounds. (📞503-585-7012; www.willametteheritage.org; 1313 Mill St SE; adult/child $8/4; 🕙10am-5pm Mon-Sat)

Mount Angel Abbey MONASTERY

6 👁 MAP P142, F1

Open to everyone, the Mount Angel Abbey is a delightful Benedictine monastery on grassy grounds set atop a hill that overlooks town. There's a modernist library designed by Finnish architect Alvar Aalto, plus a quirky museum featuring a 2.5lb pig hairball and deformed calves (among other amazing taxidermy). Lodging is available to those seeking a spiritual retreat, and the monks brew their own Belgian-style beers at Benedictine Brewery (p147), adjacent to the abbey grounds. (📞503-845-3030; www.mountangelabbey.org; 1 Abbey Dr; 🕙9am-5pm)

Mount Angel AREA

7 👁 MAP P142, F1

Eighteen miles north of Salem, the little town of Mount Angel, with its Bavarian-style storefronts and lovely abbey, is like an old-world holdover in the Oregon countryside. Visit in mid- to late September, during **Oktoberfest** (www.oktoberfest.org; day passes $5-15), for maximum effect; thousands show up for the music, beer and dances. Gothic-like **St Mary Parish Church** (1910) is worth a visit for its mural-covered walls. (www.mtangel.org)

Enchanted Forest AMUSEMENT PARK

8 👁 MAP P142, B6

Located 7 miles south of Salem, this children's theme park is a fun fantasyland offering rides (extra charge), a European village, a Western town and storybook themes, among other things. There are water light shows and a comedy theater in summer. Picnic grounds, gift shops and food services are also here. Opening hours vary widely so check the website for details. (📞503-371-4242; www.enchantedforest.com; 8462 Enchanted Way SE; adult/child $13.50/12, ride tickets $1; 🕙10am-4pm, longer hours in summer)

Bush's Pasture Park PARK

9 👁 MAP P142, B4

One of Oregon's leading citizens of the late 19th century was Asahel Bush, a newspaperman and highly successful banker who began building his rambling Italianate residence in 1877. Designed to be a self-sufficient farm, the grounds are now preserved as Bush's Pasture Park and include a large rose garden, a playground, picnic areas and walking trails. (890 Mission St SE)

Elsinore Theatre HISTORIC BUILDING

10 👁 MAP P142, B2

This dazzling Tudor-Gothic landmark, opened in 1926 and once a silent-movie theater, is now primarily a venue for theater and concerts. Classic movies are shown weekly from October to May, with live accompaniment (for silent movies) on a 1778-pipe Wurlitzer organ – one of the finest in the country. Tours by appointment. (☑503-375-3574; www.elsinoretheatre.com; 170 High St SE)

Oregon State Capitol

NOTABLE BUILDING

11 MAP P142, C2

The state's first capitol building burned down in 1855, and a domed classic Roman edifice was built to replace it. Unfortunately, that building also burned down (in 1935), and the current capitol building was completed in 1938. Bauhaus and art deco influences are apparent, especially in the strident bas-relief in the front statuary and the hatbox-like cupola. The building is faced with white Danby Vermont marble, and the interior is lined with rose travertine from Montana. (☑503-986-1388; www.oregonlegislature.gov; 900 Court St NE; admission free; ☺8am-5pm Mon-Fri)

Breitenbush Hot Springs

HOT SPRINGS

12 ◎ MAP P142, F6

Enjoy salubrious climes at Breitenbush Hot Springs, a fancy spa with massages, yoga and the like. Day-use activities include the hot springs and sauna, yoga and meditation, massage, hiking trails and a library. You can also stay the night here. Reservations are required, including for day use. (☑503-854-3320; www.breitenbush.com; 53000 Breitenbush Rd; day use per person

$23-39, children under 3 free; ☺office 9am-4pm Mon-Sat)

Willamette Valley Vineyards

WINE

13 ◎ MAP P142, B6

One of Oregon's most-respected wine growers is Willamette Valley Vineyards, on an imposing hilltop south of town. (☑503-588-9463; www.wvv.com; 8800 Enchanted Way; flights $10-15; ☺11am-6pm Sun-Thu, to 8pm Fri & Sat)

Eating

Word of Mouth Bistro

BISTRO $

14 ✗ MAP P142, B4

If crème brûlée French toast sounds good, then make a beeline for this friendly and excellent bistro. Other tasty treats include cinnamon roll pancakes, an asparagus and Brie omelet, toasted breakfast burritos and a filet mignon Benedict. Gourmet sandwiches, salads and burgers rule the lunch menu (weekdays only). (☑503-930-4285; www.wordofsalem.com; 140 17th St NE; mains $9-16; ☺7am-3pm Wed-Sun)

Wild Pear

DELI $

15 ✗ MAP P142, B1

A popular deli, Wild Pear serves up tasty soups, sandwiches and salads, along with fancier options like a lobster melt. There's also a Greek wrap, a charcuterie plate, pizzas, homemade pastries and even a traditional pho (Vietnamese noodle soup) – all combined with good, efficient service. (☎503-378-7515; www.wildpearcatering.com; 372 State St; mains $11-15; ⏱10:30am-6:30pm Mon-Sat)

Drinking

Santiam Brewing BREWERY

16 🍺 MAP P142, B4

Fans of British brews and bites should head to this lively taproom tucked in a nondescript industrial complex. Santiam has a dedicated cask-ale bar and slings craft beers and ciders along with a full menu of British and American pub fare. Expect scotch eggs, Welsh rarebit, shepherd's pie and spotted dick, plus burgers, a Philly cheesesteak and poutine. (☎503-689-1260; www. santiambrewing.com; 2544 19th St SE; pub food mains $13-16; ⏱11am-10pm Sun-Wed, to 11pm Thu-Sat)

Benedictine Brewery BREWERY

17 🍺 MAP P142, F1

At Benedictine, 18 miles northeast of Salem, the monks of Mount Angel Abbey (p145) brew Belgian-style beers using centuries-old monastic traditions. One of three monk-operated breweries in the country, they use water drawn from the abbey well and hops that have grown on the grounds since the 1880s. The brewery's serene Saint Michael's Taproom was constructed by volunteers using Douglas Fir timber from the abbey's tree farm. (☎971-343-2772; www. benedictinebrewery.com; 400 Humpert Lane; ⏱2-7pm Wed & Thu, 1-8pm Fri & Sat, 11am-5pm Sun)

Silver Falls State Park (p144)

Survival Guide

Before You Go

Book Your Stay

o Plan on paying extra (at least $25 per day) for parking at downtown and Lloyd Center hotels.

o Rates at top-end hotels vary depending on day of the week.

o Reservations are a good idea in summer.

o There's a handful of hostels and atmospheric guesthouses in more residential areas.

Useful Websites

Travel Portland (www. travelportland.com) Lists lodging options by district.

Shift Vacation Rentals (www.shiftvacation rentals.com) Local-run vacation rental homes.

Lonely Planet (www. lonelyplanet.com/usa/ pacific-northwest/port land) Recommenda-tions and bookings.

Best Budget

The Society Hotel (www.thesociety hotel.com) Bunks with

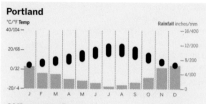

When to Go

o Portland's **summer** (June to September) sees festivals galore, including the Oregon Brewers Festival and the Bite of Oregon.

o Enjoy museums, galleries and coffee

shops during the **rainy season** (October to March).

o Long-awaited **spring** flowers reach peak bloom between April and May.

boutique style in Old Town Chinatown.

Hawthorne Portland Hostel (www.portland hostel.org) Ecofriendly, with a great Hawthorne location.

White Eagle (www.mc menamins.com/white-eagle-saloon-hotel) Supposedly haunted saloon with charm.

Friendly Bike Guest-house (www.friendly bikeguesthouse.com) Bike-friendly digs in a historic house.

Best Midrange

Ace Hotel (www.ace hotel.com/portland) Super stylish with an underground bar.

Benson Hotel (www. bensonhotel.com) Elegant downtown hotel with top-notch service.

Crystal Hotel (www. mcmenamins.com/ crystal-hotel) Themed rooms dedicated to the creatives who per-formed at the neighbor-ing Crystal Ballroom.

Kennedy School (www.mcmenamins. com/kennedy-school) Sleep in a classroom in this former elementary school.

Best Top End

Woodlark (www.wood larkhotel.com) Two his-toric buildings became one for this ultra-chic downtown boutique.

Heathman Hotel
(www.heathmanhotel.
com) Centrally located,
with luxurious design
and an impressive
library.

Lion & the Rose (www.
lionrose.com) Stately
B&B in a quiet, historic
neighborhood.

Hoxton (www.the
hoxton.com) Super-hip
design and good bars,
priced on the lower
end of the boutique
spectrum.

Arriving in Portland

Portland International Airport

Portland International Airport (📞 503-460-4234; www.flypdx.com;
7000 NE Airport Way; 📶;
🚇 Red) is located about
10 miles northeast of
downtown. There are
direct flights and connections to most major
airports in the country,
plus some direct international flights.

Union Station

Amtrak departs
from **Union Station**
(📞 800-872-7245; www.

amtrak.com; 800 NW 6th
Ave; 🚇 17, 🚇 Green, Yellow),
and offers services up
and down the West
Coast, plus a cross-
continental line.

Greyhound Depot

Greyhound buses leave
from this **depot** (Map
p88; 📞 503-243-2361;
www.greyhound.com; 550
NW 6th Ave; 🚇 Green, Orange, Yellow) and connect
Portland with cities
along I-5 and I-84.

If you're traveling
between Portland,
Seattle and Vancouver,
BC, try **Bolt Bus** (Map
p72; 📞 877-265-8287; www.
boltbus.com), which provides service in large
buses with wi-fi.

Getting Around

Bicycle

Portland is often
named the most bike-
friendly city in the US.

Check out **Everybody's Bike Rentals & Tours** (Map p88; 📞 503-358-0152; www.pdxbike
rentals.com; 305 NE Wygant
St; rentals per hour $8-25;
⏰ 10am-5pm; 🚇 6). For
city bike maps, see

www.portlandoregon.
gov/transportation.

Portland's bike-
share program is
Biketown (www.
biketownpdx.com).
After a set-up fee
of $5, the rate is 8¢
a minute, with a $2
charge for locking it at
any public rack inside
the system area ($10
if locked anywhere
outside the system). If
you return the bike to
a kiosk, you earn a $1
credit. There's an app
available for locating
bikes and making easy
payments.

Bus

The **TriMet** (www.tri
met.org) bus system
has 84 lines through
Portland. Interactive
schedules and maps
are available on the
website, and TriMet's
tracker app lets you
see details for every
bus stop in the city in
real time.

Car & Motorcycle

Parking on the east
side of the city is generally easy; downtown,
SmartPark garages,
some with electric-
vehicle charging stations, offer affordable
parking (see www.

portlandoregon.gov/transportation/35272). Downtown, Northwest and the Pearl District often have metered parking; finding a spot here can be harder.

It only became legal to pump your own gasoline in Oregon in 2019. Most stations have free full-serve attendants on-site.

Major car-rental agencies have outlets downtown and at the airport. **car2go** (www.car2go.com; membership fee $5, rental per hour from $19) and **Zipcar** (www.zipcar.com; membership fee per month from $7, rental per hour from $8.50) are popular car-sharing options.

Northwest Motorcycle Adventures (☏503-995-6962; www.northwestmotorcycleadventures.com; bike/gear rental per day $150/35; ☺by appointment) rents motorcycles and gear and also arranges tours.

Taxi

Cabs are available 24 hours by phone. **Broadway Cab** (☏503-333-3333; www.broadwaycab.com) and **Radio Cab** (☏503-227-1212; www.radiocab.net) are two reliable operators. Rideshare services are abundant.

Train

The MAX light rail connects to most of the major metro areas (and suburbs) and are easily navigable. Buses connect with many stops.

The Portland Street Car runs downtown and near the river on the eastern side. For maps and trip planning for all of these, download the app for TriMet.

Essential Information

Accessible Travel

Portland in general is widely accessible for travelers with disabilities; for information on getting around town by light rail or bus, call ☏503-962-2455 or email accessible@trimet.org.

To increase access to cycling, Biketown has a program called **Adaptive Biketown** (www.adaptivebiketown.com) that rents hand- and foot-powered recumbent bikes through a local agency.

Inside the **Travel Portland** (Map p38; ☏503-275-8355; www.travelportland.com; 701 SW 6th Ave; ☺8:30am-5:30pm Mon-Fri, 10am-4pm Sat Nov-Apr, plus 10am-2pm Sun May-Oct; ☒Red, Blue, Green, Yellow) visitor center at Pioneer Courthouse Square, there's a high-tech, all-gender, ADA-accessible restroom with an attendant on duty.

Download Lonely Planet's free Accessible Travel guides from http://lptravel.to/AccessibleTravel.

Business Hours

The following hours are a general guide – check individual listings for specifics.

Restaurants Breakfast 7am to 11:30am, lunch 11:30am to 2pm, dinner 5 to 9pm

Shops 9am to 5pm (malls to 9pm) Monday to Friday; sometimes more limited hours on weekends

Banks 9am or 10am to 5pm or 6pm weekdays; some also 10am to 2pm Saturday

Supermarkets 7am to 10pm; sometimes 24-hr

Discount Cards
Student discounts
School ID cards may enable discounts on admission to attractions.

HI-USA card (www. hiusa.org) Two Portland hostels, Northwest Portland Hostel (www. nwportlandhostel. com) and Hawthorne Portland Hostel (www. portlandhostel.org), are members of HI-USA, which is affiliated with Hostelling International. A HI-USA can save a few bucks and are available for purchase at check-in.

Military and senior discounts Many establishments offer discounts for active and retired military personnel, as well as people aged over 60 – just show any form of government-issued identification.

Family Fun Pass (www. familyfunpass.org) Enables discounted access to attractions around Portland and the Willamette Valley. Passes start at $49 for a group of four.

Electricity

Type A
120V/60Hz

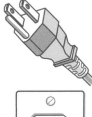

Type B
120V/60Hz

Important Holidays
New Year's Day
January 1

Martin Luther King Jr Day Third Monday in January

Presidents' Day Third Monday in February

Easter March/April

Memorial Day Last Monday in May

LGBTQ+ Pride Third weekend following Memorial Day

Independence Day (Fourth of July) July 4

Labor Day First Monday in September

Indigenous People's Day Second Monday in October

Halloween October 31

Veterans' Day November 11

Thanksgiving Day Fourth Thursday in November

Christmas Day December 25

New Year's Eve December 31

LGBTQ+ Travelers
Portland is home to the second-largest LGBTQ+ community in the US (second to San Francisco).

However, bias crimes (especially towards transgender and non-binary people) do still occur. Local alt-right political groups have been known to incite terror among the city's LGBT+ contingent.

Money

ATMs are abundant. Many bars, restaurants and grocery stores also have them, but fees are steep ($3 to $5, plus your own bank's fees).

There is a **Travelex** (Map p38; 503-227-1104; 321 SW 6th Ave; 9am-5pm Mon-Fri) downtown and at Portland International Airport.

Exchange Rates

Australia	A$1	$0.69
Canada	C$1	$0.76
China	¥1	$0.14
EU	€1	$1.10
Japan	¥100	$0.92
NZ	NZ$1	$0.64
UK	£1	$1.23

For current exchange rates, visit www.xe.com.

Tipping

Tipping in the US is *not* optional, as most service-industry workers make only the minimum wage and rely almost entirely on tips for their income. However, if service is truly terrible, tip less than 15% or reduce the following standard amounts.

Bartenders $1 to $2 per drink, or 15% of the bill. Note: good tippers get stronger drinks.

Bellhops $2 per bag, plus $5 to $10 extra for special service.

Housekeeping staff $2 to $5 daily, left on the pillow each day; more if you're messy.

Parking valets $2; extra for special service.

Restaurant servers 15% to 20% of the pretax bill.

Taxis and rideshares 10% to 15% of the metered fare.

Toilets

Toilets are easy to find in Portland – shops and restaurants usually require a purchase.

There is an 11-stall restroom inside the Travel Portland visitor center.

Tourist Information

Travel Portland (Map p38; 503-275-8355; www.travelportland.com; 701 SW 6th Ave, Pioneer Courthouse Sq; 8:30am-5:30pm Mon-Fri, 10am-4pm Sat Nov-Apr, plus 10am-2pm Sun May-Oct; Red, Blue, Green, Yellow) Has superfriendly volunteers staffing this office. There's a small theater with a 12-minute film about the city, and there are **TriMet** (Map p38; 503-725-9005, 503-238-7433; www.trimet.org; 8:30am-5:30pm Mon-Fri) bus and light-rail offices inside.

Visas

For up-to-date information about visas and immigration, check the US Department of State (www.travel.state.gov) and the travel section of US Customs & Border Protection (www.cbp.gov).

Most foreign visitors need a visa to enter the US. You can determine your eligibility for a Waiver of Tourist Visa (VWT) with the Electronic System for Travel Authorization (ESTA; www.cbp.gov/travel/international-visitors/esta). Visitors should carry their passport (valid for at least six months) and expect to be photographed and have their index fingers scanned.

Behind the Scenes

Send Us Your Feedback

We love to hear from travelers – your comments help make our books better. We read every word, and we guarantee that your feedback goes straight to the authors. Visit **lonelyplanet.com/contact** to submit your updates and suggestions.

Note: We may edit, reproduce and incorporate your comments in Lonely Planet products such as guidebooks, websites and digital products, so let us know if you don't want your comments reproduced or your name acknowledged. For a copy of our privacy policy visit lonelyplanet.com/privacy.

Celeste's Thanks

Thanks to my husband Josh and my kids who have come with me on so many Oregon trips over the years. And to many friends old and new that helped out this time around, including Ticari, Chris and Ashley, Nathan, Dana, Jon and Kara, Ron and Nisa, Elizabeth, Pattye, Rachel Cabakoff, Amanda Castleman, Dave Nevins, Amy Hunter, all my LP co-authors and Ben Buckner for seeing through.

Acknowledgements

Cover photograph: Portland skyline with Mt Hood in the distance, Sean Pavone/Alamy Stock Photo ©

Image p34: *Allow Me* by Seward Johnson © 1981 The Seward Johnson Atelier, Inc. The Seward Johnson Atelier is devoted to bringing art into the public realm, available to all. sewardjohnsonatelier.org

This Book

This first edition of Lonely Planet's *Pocket Portland & the Willamette Valley* guidebook was curated by Celeste Brash and researched and written by Celeste and MaSovaida Morgan. This guidebook was produced by the following:

Destination Editor
Ben Buckner

Senior Product Editors
Grace Dobell, Kathryn Rowan

Regional Senior Cartographer Alison Lyall

Product Editor
Hannah Cartmel

Book Designer
Virginia Moreno

Assisting Editors Sarah Bailey, James Bainbridge, Carly Hall, Gabrielle Innes, Lou McGregor, Monique Perrin, Sarah Reid, Gabrielle Stefanos

Cartographers
Diana Von Holdt, Julie Sheridan

Cover Researcher
Naomi Parker

Thanks to Victoria Harrison, Andi Jones, Jenna Myers, Lauren O'Connell, Vicky Smith

Index

See also separate subindexes for:
Eating p158
Drinking p159
Entertainment p159
Shopping p159

Sights 000
Map Pages **000**

3/20

Our Writers

Celeste Brash

Like many California natives, Celeste now lives in Portland. She arrived, however, after 15 years in French Polynesia, a year and a half in Southeast Asia and a stint teaching English as a second language (with an American accent) in Brighton, England – among other things. She's been writing guidebooks for Lonely Planet since 2005 and her travel articles have appeared in publications from BBC Travel to *National Geographic*. She's currently writing a book about her five years on a remote pearl farm in the Tuamotu Atolls and is represented by the Donald Maass Agency, New York.

MaSovaida Morgan

MaSovaida is a travel writer and multimedia storyteller whose wanderlust has taken her to more than 40 countries and all seven continents. Previously, she was Lonely Planet's Destination Editor for South America and Antarctica for four years and worked as an editor for newspapers and NGOs in the Middle East and United Kingdom. Follow her on Instagram @MaSovaida.

Published by Lonely Planet Global Limited
CRN 554153
1st edition – February 2020
ISBN 978 1 78868 275 6
© Lonely Planet 2020 Photographs © as indicated 2020
10 9 8 7 6 5 4 3 2 1
Printed in Singapore